AF304772

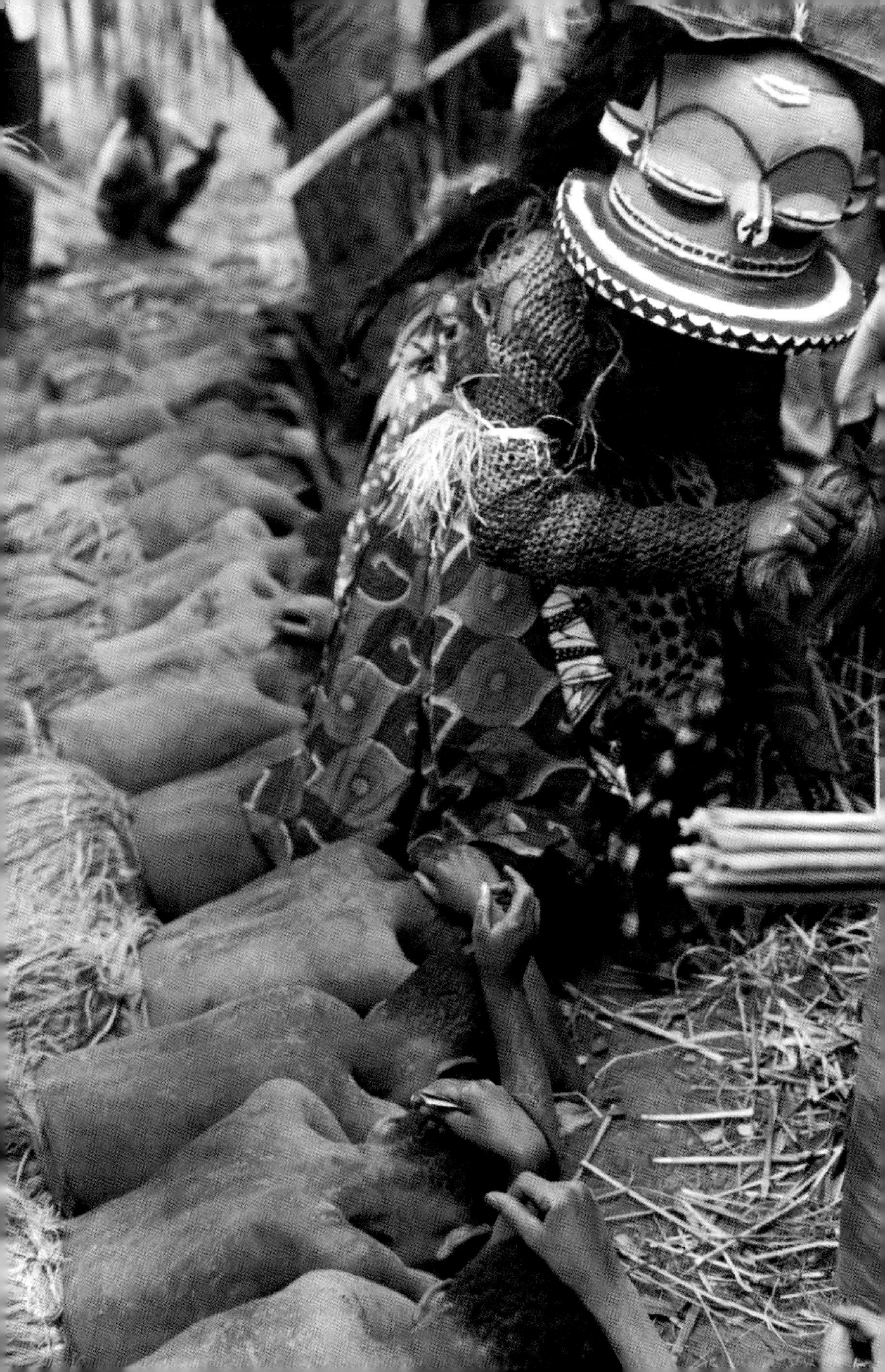

Z. S. Strother

PENDE

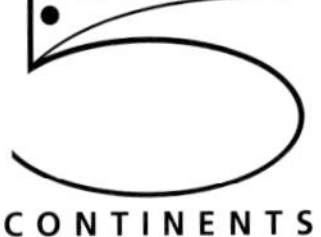

For Henry Goertz, who got me back to Pendeland

Editorial Coordination
Alessandra Chioetto

Editing
Timothy Stroud

Art Director
Fayçal Zaouali

Layout
Annarita De Sanctis
Daniela Duminuco

Iconographical Research
Massimo Zanella
Marie-Laure Jouve

Acknowledgements
The publisher would especially like to thank
Marc Ghysels for his invaluable assistance
and the Royal Museum for Central Africa,
Tervuren, Belgium

The author wishes to thank the many curators
and collectors who graciously opened their
collections to the public. Anne-Marie Bouttiaux,
Alessandra Chioetto, Laurence Denié-Higney,
Marc Félix, Aurélien Gaborit, Eric Ghysels,
Gisagi Gidiongo, Marie-Laure Jouve,
Nzomba Kakema Dugo, Costa Petridis,
and Barbara Roesmann:
all made critical interventions, which allowed the
project to reach fruition.

The research and writing of this text was supported
by a Frederick Burkhardt Residential Fellowship,
sponsored by the American Council
of Learned Societies, and the University
of California, Los Angeles.

ISBN 978-88-7439-384-8

First published in Italy in January 2008 by
5 Continents Editions
Via Cosimo del Fante, 13
20122 Milan
www.fivecontinentseditions.com

Cover
Mbangu (Pl. 18). Royal Museum for Central Africa,
Tervuren.

Back cover
The mask and the whip are emblems
for the boys' initiation (*mukanda*).
Kisonji, DRC★, 1987. Photo: Z. S. Strother

Page 2
The Kipoko mask supervises a ritual during Chief
Kende's boys' initiation into the men's fraternity.
Ndjindji, DRC, 1987. Photograph: Z. S. Strother

★ Apart from its first occurence in the text, the
abreviation DRC has been used for the Democratic
Republic of Congo.

Table of Contents

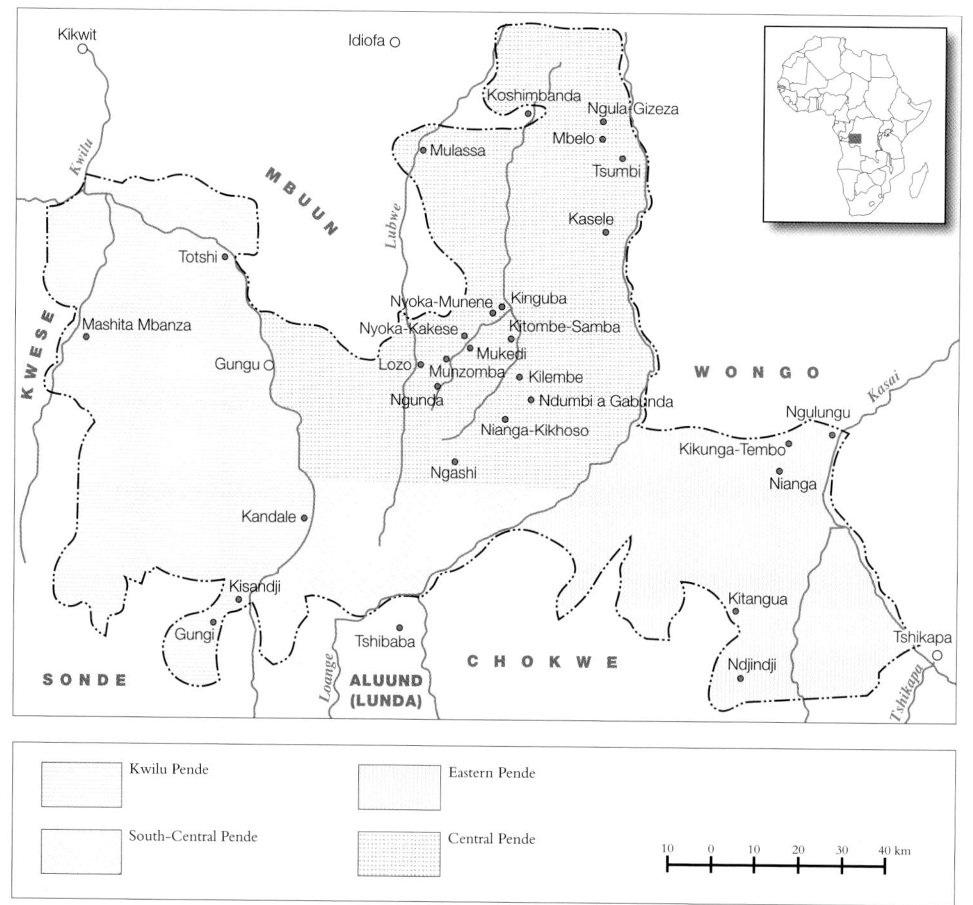

Map of Pende territory in the Democratic Republic of the Congo (DRC)

The Experience of Art

Introduction

Twentieth-century oral history attributes Pende origins to refugees who fled incorporation into Queen Njinga's and other predatory Angolan states in the seventeenth century. These groups moved north to form small, autonomous chiefdoms in the grasslands of what is today south-central Democratic Republic of the Congo (DRC). Although colonial and postcolonial regimes have layered state structures over these autonomous chiefdoms, local practice has continued to undermine the consolidation of political power. Several historians have argued that opposition to centralized authority is a deep-rooted cultural trait that has shaped Pende history over the past several hundred years (Kodi 1976, 1: 164-65; Sikitele 1986: 118).

A significant body of African art literature since the 1960s has been oriented towards kingdoms, where the arts are presumed both to reflect and reinforce the ideology of the ruling élite. In contrast, the Pende provide a window into social contexts where the arts become vehicles to contest power and renegotiate relationships. Thus, this essay examines the interplay between masquerader and audience, object and observer, the living and the dead, the community and its chief, the colonised and coloniser. It has also been a priority to demonstrate the ability of individual works to evoke a range of aesthetic responses based on contextual frame and viewer's subject position, both of which necessarily change over time.

Although the essay addresses a broad range of Pende visual culture, it opens with masquerade because the vitality of this institution has influenced almost all of the other branches of the arts. In particular, masquerade proved resilient during the Belgian colonial occupation, 1908-1960, when many of the decorative arts disappeared. Throughout this period, masquerades provided a unique space in which young men could vie for fame and where the booming drums and crowds united in song and dance spoke forcibly of an alternative identity to the one imposed by the state. They even provided a venue for covert commentary on contemporary affairs. For all these reasons, issues central to masquerade such as gender, physiognomy, and the politics of the gaze will emerge as critical analytical tools in discussion of everything from stools to pendants.

The continuing importance of masquerade to Pende experience was confirmed during 32 months of fieldwork, 1987-89, during which I observed 26 days of village masquerading and over 133 days of initiation masquerading when I was able to attend two boys' initiations (*mukanda*) in different regions from beginning to end. A short follow-up visit in 2006 confirmed that the *mukanda* and sculpture associated with the chief's ritual house are still remarkably vital among the Eastern Pende.

In terminology, I respect Pende usage in referring to the headdress, as well as to the persona created through the combination of headdress, costume and performance, as a "mask" (*mbuya*). In Kipende, one speaks of "dancing a mask" (*kukina mbuya*), never "wearing" it.

This text is deeply indebted to the work of Léon de Sousberghe, S.J., who carefully documented Pende art from 1907 to 1957 (1959: 2). Drawing on fieldwork from 1951-53 and 1955-57, he concluded that one must discard the idea of a single, homogenous Pende style and recognise a multitude of local centres (1959: 10, 21-27). The earliest collections of Pende art, made by Emil Torday in 1905 and 1909, by Leo Frobenius in 1905, and by Frederick Starr in 1905-06, demonstrate that strikingly individual regional styles were fully developed at the beginning of the twentieth-century. While earlier texts distinguished between the "Western" and "Eastern" Pende (separated by the Loange River), I have argued that culturally it makes more sense to speak of four regions: "Kwilu Pende" (west of the Kwilu River); "Central Pende" (north of Ngashi, sandwiched between the Kwilu and Loange Rivers); "South-Central Pende"; and "Eastern Pende" (sandwiched between the Loange and Kasai Rivers) (Strother 1998: 6-8).

The objects were selected to suggest the variety and richness of twentieth-century visual practice but also because they are capable of nourishing discussion of audience reception. As much as possible, I have tried to acknowledge the works as individual interpretations rather than illustrations of generic "types". In the end, recovery of social context, patronage, the conditions for viewing, and audience response enable one to construct a "cultural biography" (Kopytoff 1986) for the arts, which demonstrates their importance to twentieth-century experience.

THE MASK AND THE SWITCH

One day during the boys' initiation into the men's fraternity (*mukanda*) in 1987, a group of Eastern Pende masqueraders caught five or six teenage girls on their way to wash dishes at the spring in a large clearing. Shrieking,

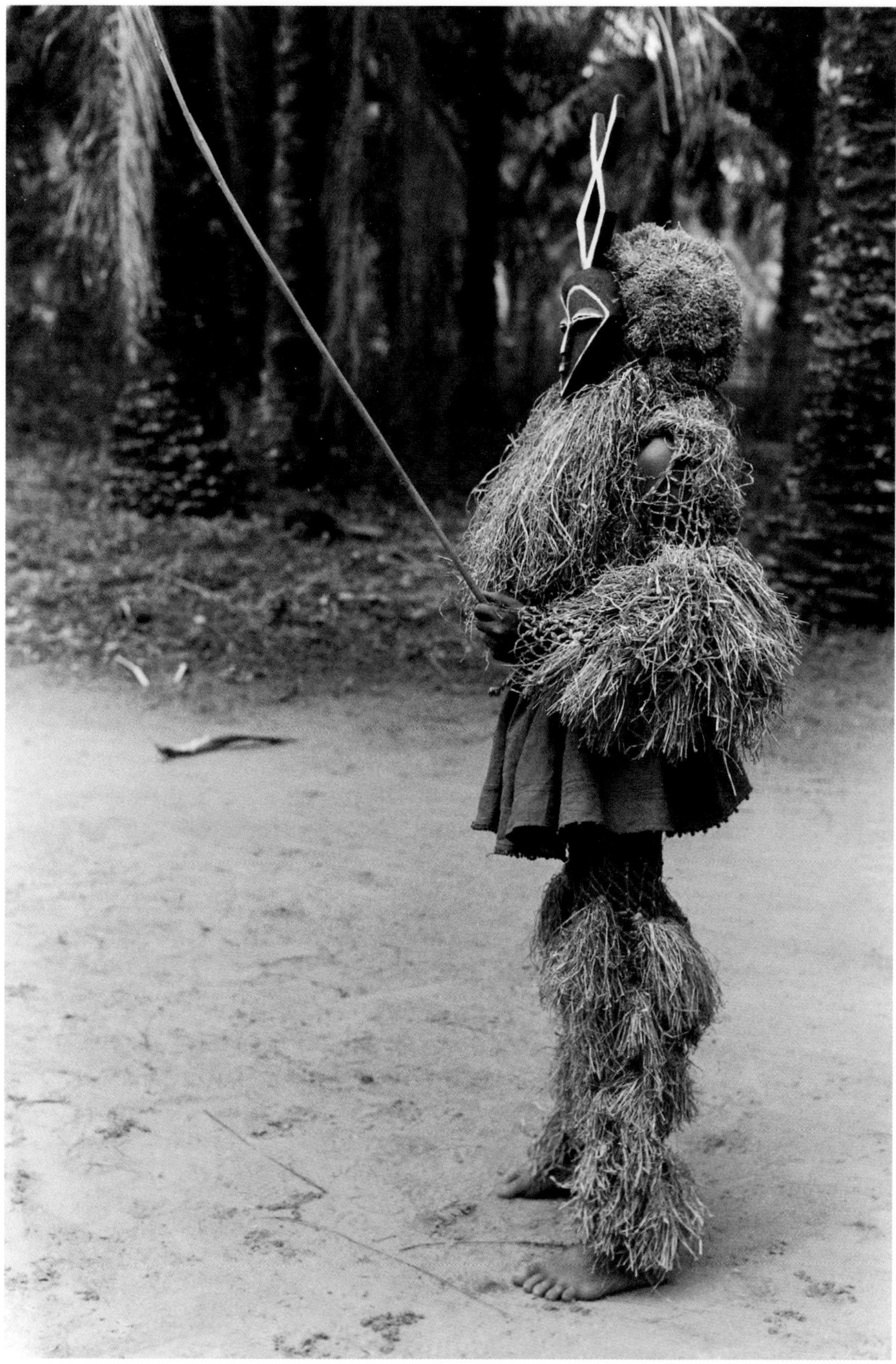

Fig. 1. The mask and the switch are emblems for the boys' initiation (*mukanda*).
Chief Kisonji carved the mask Thangi for a camp in 1987. DRC. Photo: Z. S. Strother

the girls clustered together, turning their backs to the maskers who slashed at their legs with whips. Since the chief sponsoring this particular initiation had maintained tight rules about the use of switches, and because the boys were good-natured, the slashes were largely for show. However, these young girls had been caught off guard and were petrified. Several dropped the enamel basins that they were carrying on their heads and their dishes clattered onto the ground. Delighted with their success, the masks ran off into the high grass.

Women, children, and visitors from neighbouring communities constitute the primary audience for Central African masquerades. During the initiation, masqueraders erupt daily from the tall grass ("the bush") into the village. They carry switches cut from branches, which can draw blood [fig. 1]. Nevertheless, there are many rules about whom they may strike. As a courtesy, no one may whip the wife of a chief, sculptor, blacksmith, master drummer, singer, or dancer because these men's skills make masquerades possible. No one may hit any middle-aged woman, *unless* they have sons in the camp. And certainly, no one may hit little girls, grandmothers, or anyone carrying a baby. The main targets are mothers of initiates, adolescent girls, and uninitiated boys.

Moreover, it is forbidden to hit all strangers. Masks often travel to other communities for dancing, but they may only strike someone in a neighbour's village if that person belongs to the same clan. *This means that the victims know their persecutors.* Unlike Mardi Gras celebrations around the world, where thousands of revellers pour into cities and depend upon their anonymity, Pende masquerading exploits an intimate relationship between the masker and audience. A better analogy would be with the kind of masquerading once common in villages in Switzerland and Central Europe.

For the audience, part of the masquerade lies in quickly processing who might be stalking them, looking for clues in the masqueraders' relative size, body language, and exposed hands and feet [fig.1]. Can they figure out if it is a friend or brother who will only tease? Or is it the local bully who would like nothing better than to draw blood? Is it a stranger, who may charge but who will always veer off without contact? Or is it a son, who misses his mother and is taking this opportunity to show off for her, hoping that she will guess who he is? For both, this is a poignant moment. I have seen mothers simultaneously smiling and teary-eyed after such encounters. While it reassures her to see her son healthy and mischievous, she cannot help feeling a little sad that she may not touch him or address him by name.

Think about this woman's experience. She knows who it is. Or does she? Is she certain enough to risk being switched? And even if she is sure, the familiar person now seems different since he is silent and behaving strangely.

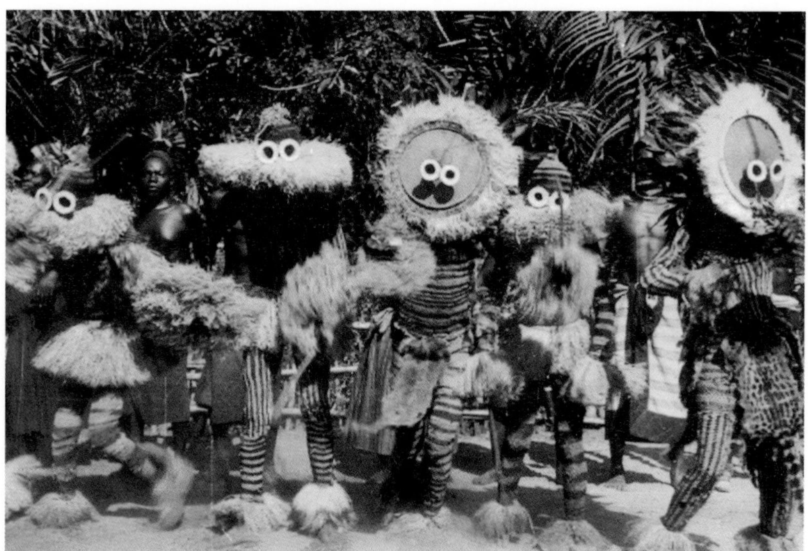

Fig. 2. Kwilu Pende. Minganji Group in Gungu. Photo: A. Scohy, 1950,
Royal Museum for Central Africa, Tervuren, EPH. 11531

The experience of proximity and separation drives home the reality that
her son has moved beyond her domain into the realm of men. Part of what
makes the masquerading experience so powerful in small communities is
the wide range of emotions that can be aroused.

There are additional rules that ensure a raucous atmosphere reminiscent
of "tag", where the would-be victims taunt the masqueraders before they
dash to safety. Masks may never appear at night. Masqueraders may never
enter houses, so sprinting women and children often slam doors in their
faces. Frustrated, the maskers will kick the doors as hard as they can to suggest that this once they might not follow the rules. Inside, the inhabitants
watch the door jump on its hinges with bated breath, suddenly anxious that
it might not hold. Women and children caught out in the open may also
grab onto one of the many exempted men or women for safety. However,
every initiation season there are trials over boys who hit too hard or break
the rules respecting safe zones. The violators face heavy penalties, but the fact
that boys can be counted on to be impulsive means that an aura of uncer-
tainty surrounds the mask.

Communities also have distinct personalities. Many struggle to maintain
a playful tone in the interactions between women and masks. However,
masks always have the potential for violence and sadistic personalities profit
from the suspension of normal social conventions to wound and intimidate.
One friend was terrified because she knew that a rejected suitor was shadowing

her. Nyange would hide in her house each day until late in the day (whereas women usually like to go farming early in the morning before the sun grows hot). During the long walk to the fields, she would hurry, listening intently for any tell-tale rustle.

In fact, people usually hear the masks before they see them. The masqueraders are required to carry rattles. Moreover, as creatures of the bush, their costumes incorporate masses of raffia threads, which rustle noisily. As a result, even the masquerader's shuffling walk creates a distinctive sound that once heard is never forgotten. Since it is difficult to take anyone unaware, masks must resort to cunning. They like to hide behind buildings or shrubs to ambush their prey, but it is rare for them to be able to surprise their targets as they did the girls on their way to the spring, who were laughing and oblivious to their surroundings.

The sensation of hearing masks before being able to locate them is an important feature of the masquerading experience. It heightens the viewers' sense of vulnerability. One becomes self-conscious of being watched while yet unable to see. This is always a creepy sensation but even more so in a context where the observer carries a whip.

The headdresses of masks often exteriorise the gaze and query: *who has the right to look at whom?* In Figure 1, the masker bears the slit-eyed gaze associated with women, which creates a false sense of security: "Come closer, I'm harmless, I don't see very well". Lured into proximity, the viewer may be caught by the switch. In this context, audience members speak of the masquerader's duplicity and cunning. More often, *mukanda* masks flaunt their aggression through their incorporation of wide-open, white-rimmed eyes, which Pende associate with unleashed anger. Such eyes warn about the reversal of roles where the subject has become the object; the viewer, the viewed. In particular, the *mukanda* masks of the Central and Kwilu Pende (called *Minganji* or *Tungolo*) are all about the gaze [fig. 2]. Their large, staring eyes grow larger as they protrude into space.

Masks are tools of estrangement, which permit their audience to see familiar people and spaces differently. By rendering that audience self-conscious, they even provoke a changed experience of self. John Rudlin (a theorist of *Commedia dell'Arte*) counsels actors: "A real mask should never be hung on a wall, unless its working days are over, since its gaze will be diminished by unanimated familiarity" (1994: 40). He raises a critical question: how to keep the mask's uncanny presence from being neutralised by over-familiarity? As Rudlin indicates, probably the most common technique is to shroud it in long periods of invisibility. The Pende case is complex. Although initiation masks appear only about once every decade, they perform daily for a period of eight to ten weeks. During this period, they preserve their aura through their unpredictability as they ricochet between comedy and terror. Even a chief, sculptor, or blacksmith, who knows that his position is inviolable, experiences a jolt of fear vicariously when he is knocked off balance by the tackle of frantic relatives who grab at him as a "safety" as they sprint ahead of the switch. Even if a woman has never been chased personally, she knows that it is possible and this hangs in the air. When children dream of masks, they are always nightmares. For adults, a tell-tale rattle reawakens momentarily the reflexes of childhood.

In Europe and the United States, scholars describe the museum as one of the primary sites for socialising contemporary audiences towards a reverence for art (Duncan 1995). The temple-like structure, the dim interior, the special spot-lighting on works isolated one from the other, and the hushed voices and muted children, all influence how visitors respond to the objects contained within. Consistent modes of display underplay and even disguise significant differences among objects from different cultures and historical periods, thereby permitting claims to timeless and universal truth.

I would argue that masquerade comprises a primary site for socialisation to the arts among the Pende. In contrast to the museum, Nzomba Kakema Dugo argues that masquerade sensitises viewers to context since where and how one confronts a mask entail such different consequences. Masks teach the viewer to pay attention, never to take them for granted, lest they catch one unawares. Masks also sensitise their audience to the politics of the gaze, who may look at whom, and when or where the rules may change. Meanings shift dramatically according to subject position. At the very least, every adult has experienced a changing relationship with the masks as he or she ages.

Unmasking

The Eastern Pende initiation (*mukanda*) is partly boot camp, puberty ritual, woods and crafts camp, and school. Its purpose is to socialise the boys for their eventual role as men in society. The request to hold an initiation must come from the boys themselves. In theory and usually in practice, all boys must go voluntarily to *mukanda* [fig. 3]. Although initiates ranged from eight to twenty-three in camps, 1987-88, the average age was fourteen. Pushed by the desire to be classified as an adult, one or several boys went into the bush and announced their request in song: "Fathers, why are you silent? [The mask] Ngolo arrives!" They also tried to shame their peers into joining them: "Whoever stays in the village is a little boy! May his mother beat him with her cooking spoon!" The rule of thumb was that if the youngster had the courage to face his childhood terror, the whip-toting fraternity masks, he was ready.

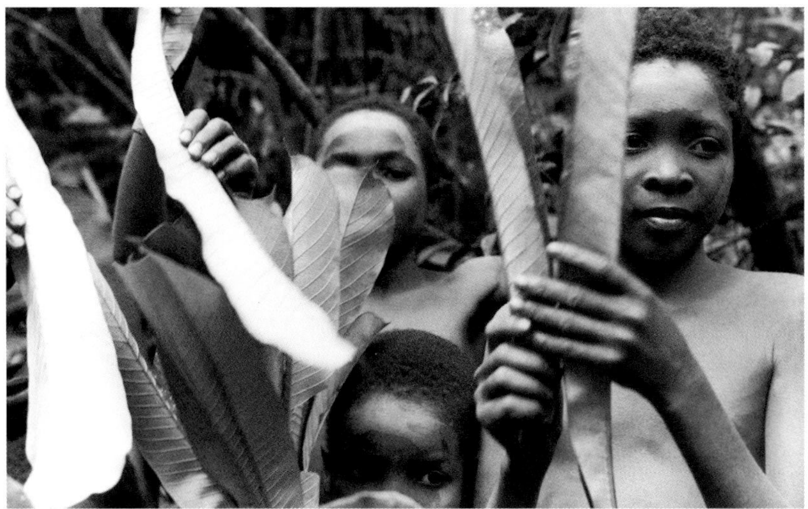

Fig. 3. Eastern Pende respect a boy's decision to seek initiation even when
(as in the case of Kidinda, on the right) his parents resist. Ndjindji, DRC, 1987.
Photo: Z. S. Strother

When the community accepts the boys' petition, the first task for the
chief will be to commission a new series of fraternity masks from a professional sculptor. Some of the most recent graduates are also galvanised to make
costumes. In the weeks ahead, older initiates will sculpt additional headpieces
according to their talents. These works must be carved afresh for each generation, never inherited, as a gift of love and sacrifice.

The initiation opens and closes with rituals of unmasking. On the tenth
day of Chief Kende's *mukanda*, in 1987, there were finally enough masks
and costumes to begin. Dozens of young men gathered on the outskirts of the
camp, all armed with switches. The boys could spy five horned masks cavort-
ing in the distance. The masqueraders raised clouds of dust as they lunged at
each other, shaking their horns, stamping and pirouetting. One mask was distinguished from the others by wearing an overskirt of long, shiny, green
leaves. The mask who wears this over-skirt will serve as Ngolo. The term *ngolo*
conveys all that the initiation is supposed to secure for the boys, literally
signifying "strength", hence by extension "health" and male potency. The
familiar green leaves symbolise the dangers of touching since contact with
them can provoke itchy rashes.

The boys huddled together, transfixed in disbelief. Chief Kende exhorted
them: "Don't be afraid! Don't be distracted! Concentrate!" Their fathers
explained that they must now do what had always been forbidden: they must
launch themselves at Ngolo and rip off its headpiece, thereby laying claim

to manhood through force of arm (*ku ngolo*). Gradually, the masks circled closer, several running defence for the mask serving as their target. Finally, Luya, a courageous 14-year-old, broke from the ranks and ran at Ngolo. The other boys followed. However, the masquerader was significantly larger than Luya and the boy was unable to dislodge his headpiece. As they grappled, another mask prepared to give Luya a wicked blow across the back with his whip. Luya's father, enraged, charged up to protect his son, blocking the blow, and helping the boy tear off the mask.

At this point, the clearing became the site of a general mêlée, where many of the fathers struggled with the masqueraders, who slashed at the older men to protect themselves. Although unscripted, the initiation is almost always marked by brawls between the fathers of initiates and the youngest generation of graduates, who grow overly enthusiastic about their rights to enforce discipline. During this period, many fathers hover protectively over their sons and their concern reinforces strong bonds between them.

When things had quieted down, Luya's companions were not let off the hook. Each was obliged to pluck a thread from Ngolo's costume and to receive a (mild) blow from the whip. In the past, after the unmasking, the boys were circumcised (although the colonial state required this operation to take place at birth beginning in the 1930s-40s). Many Pende believe that circumcision ensures male fertility by removing all barriers to ejaculation.

During the initiation, the boys live outside of civilisation, in the bush. They must sleep on the ground and are (falsely) rumoured not to cook their food. Eastern Pende *mukanda* masks play on the idea that the initiates have become "like" creatures of the bush by fusing human and animal features. Every camp must have at least one Ngolo, which technically is a mask with two straight horns invoking generic antelope horns. In practice, the role of Ngolo may be filled by any mask with two horns. Some of the horns refer to specific animals; for example, the roan antelope, once feared for disembowelling hunters. All of the creatures cited belong to the savannah (where the boys live during this period) or the village. However, novelty is appreciated—some sculptors pun on horns, representing them as knives or swords. Others are quite fanciful. Thangi usually has zigzagging, "broken" horns but Chief Kisonji (also a sculptor) carved one in which he elegantly crossed the two horns, forming a lozenge-shape, a pattern strictly reserved to mark the possessions of chiefs [fig. 1]. Chief Kisonji thereby boasts of his "ownership" of the *mukanda*, the hosting of which comprises a prerogative once restricted to paramount chiefs.

The sculptor Ngoma Kandaku Mbuya has argued that *thangi* (an archaic word signifying "defiant and disregardful of social convention") puns on

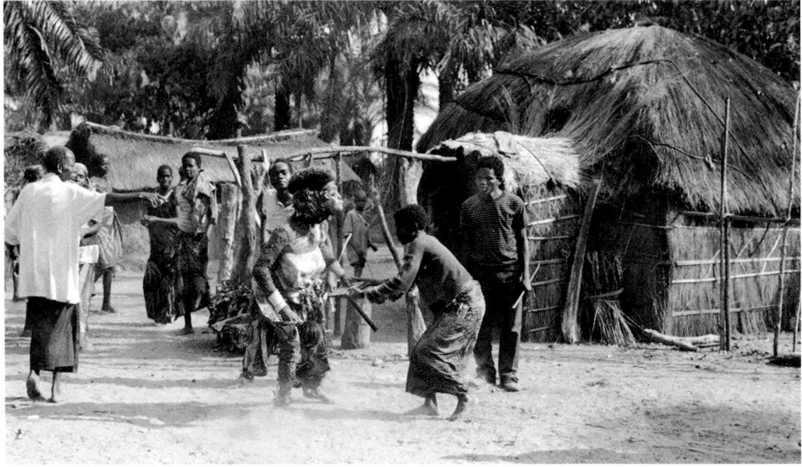

Fig. 4. One of the wives of Chief Kombo-Kiboto (Mukanzo a Kilumbu)
dances with the female mask Kambanda. Ndjindji, DRC, 1987.
Photo: Z. S. Strother

matangi ("thoughts"). For him, the zigzagging horns exhort the initiates to
resourcefulness as they confront difficulties in life. Sometimes, one must try
many different solutions (paths) before finding the best approach to a problem.
Whether or not his etymology is correct, Ngoma's thought process demonstrates the expectation that the superstructure of the mask will encode a
word of advice for the initiates: they should be strong and determined like
rams; they should show the courage of the roan antelope; they should be
cunning like the hawk *kababo*; and so forth.

After the boys have demonstrated public mastery of an impressive corpus
of fraternity songs and dances, they must turn their efforts to mastering the
dances for the village masks (*mbuya jia kifutshi*). The most important of these,
the *Lukongo*, is the dance for Kipoko, also known as Mukishi wa Mutsue or
Mbundju. (The names of masks vary regionally and change over time.) The   Pl. 8
Lukongo is the preeminent men's dance, which chiefs perform on the day of
their investiture. By learning it, every boy claims the right to become chief
and to take responsibility for the ritual needs of the community. The initiates
also will be coached on performing Pota; the young woman [fig. 4]; and maybe
others. As well as the footwork, they learn to mimic women's food prepara-   Pl. 3, 6
tion. Famed dancer Mbuka Makungu emphasised that such pantomimes
are essential to the meaning of the *Lukongo* since they offer a danced prayer,
which thanks the dead for the year's harvests and petitions future beneficence.

Near the end of the initiation, the boys are taken to a clearing. They are
lined up and each told to lie down with their right hand resting on their

heads so that they cannot see what is happening [frontispiece]. The Kipoko mask approaches, brushes a medicine on the back of each boy and steps twice on the base of each boy's spine. Then he taps the boy's head with the handle to his fly-whisk and takes the small bill each holds in the right hand to "pay" for his treatment. Since Pende believe that a man's sperm are located in a sack at the base of his spine, Kipoko's actions convey a prayer to strengthen the boys' backs and to prevent impotence.

Afterwards, Kipoko sits down on an over-turned mortar as the boys are organised in a line. At Kende, an attendant stuck a little bit of millet-cassava bread and chicken onto the end of the nose of Kipoko. In some other communities, they will place the food on the shelf provided at the base of the helmet-mask. At Kende, each boy had to take hold of the ears, reach forward and swallow the food, pivot and run back down the line as three graduates tried to whip him smartly across the back. This meal is considered a test for potential potency. If a child vomits (as happened in 1987), he will be pushed aside and will not graduate on time. Since the boys now have purchased their right to dance the *kifutshi* masks, they escort Kipoko into the village square for a general celebration. Each boy will demonstrate his command of Kipoko's dance to the warm enthusiasm of the crowd.

The most common justification for the *mukanda* is that it provides men with a secret domain of knowledge since women once restricted access to the mysteries of childbirth. The first unmasking is construed as a theft, as an act of violence that irrevocably ends childhood. By contrast, the second is framed as a purchase following a period of study and rehearsal. Laying hands on Kipoko reintegrates the boys into daily life. By learning the dances of the *kifutshi* masks, the boys are also learning to take responsibility for an important domain of religious life in the community. Men's responsibility for ritual, in particular for communication with the other world, complements women's control over childbirth.

MASKS OF JOY

Don't mix fraternity masks (*mbuya jia mukanda*)
with village masks (*mbuya jia kifutshi*)!

—Chief Kikuba

The relationship of the different kinds of masks has been a point of considerable confusion in the literature. There has been a tendency to lump all masks together since their performance is restricted to initiated men. However, field associates emphasised the differences between the two main categories. Despite their sociological significance, the whip-toting fraternity masks are universally dismissed as "police" (*pulushi*). They discipline the initiates and intimidate outsiders from approaching the camps. Among the Central and Kwilu Pende, the *Minganji* appear outside the initiation context in certain other "police" functions [fig. 2]. For example, in the late 1980s, they patrolled the woods in order to stop people from harvesting caterpillars (an important protein source) before they were fully mature. Visually, the horns, protruding eyes, ruffs of raffia, and switches all evoke danger [figs. 1, 2].

By contrast, the village masks are deemed "serious" since they help safeguard the well-being of the *kifutshi*. As a term, "*kifutshi*" embraces the entire environmental microcosm essential to the survival of any community, including the village, its people and domestic beasts, but also the fields, streams, grasslands, forests and wild game, in short, all that makes life possible. In Pende religion, God (*Maweze*) created the world and placed humans in a cycle of reincarnation in which the dead act as caretakers over their junior relatives. The world of the living is opposed to *kalunga*, the other world, located underground. Although individuals may pray to particular relatives for personal concerns, the dead have established certain tools to address issues of collective well-being. "*Mahamba*" are defined as altars "where we pray to the dead" (*kukombela vumbi*) and the term extends also to the rituals instituted by the collective dead to communicate with the living (Strother 2000a: 57-58; Delaere 1942-45: 625; de Sousberghe 1961: 63 n.2). In a telling metaphor, Chief Samba (Ngoyi Kisabu Kavundji) described *mahamba* as "transistors", which facilitate communication by amplifying the message to be delivered to the other world.

Unlike the *mukanda* masks, which chase and divide, the village masks seek to bring everyone together, the living as well as the dead, in an atmosphere of joy and thanksgiving. For this reason, they constitute particularly powerful *mahamba*, which otherwise take on a wide variety of forms. They are danced routinely before the sowing of millet or the burning of the bush but also for a chief's investiture, to close *mukanda*, or during periods of epidemic or chief's illness.

The full significance of audience reception was revealed during a masquerade for Chief Kingange in 1988. All day, the dancing had lacked enthusiasm and had been bedevilled by mishaps. To my surprise, minutes before the affair ended, Chief Nzambi, who was visiting, got up and began to perform the *Lukongo*, the signature dance for Kipoko. Suddenly, the crowd went wild. It gained all the animation that had been lacking all day. Young men and old went up to give him little gifts of money in praise. The women responded by throwing handfuls of millet, or crashing down rootstocks of

Pl. 8

manioc, or dancing with goods that they had purchased with funds deriving from the previous year's harvest. One woman trailed after him, ululating, while she twirled a newborn infant, whose feet she periodically tapped gently on the ground.

When I asked him why he had stood up to dance, Nzambi explained that he had felt sorry for me: I had come from so far away to see masquerades and the entire day had been flat because the Kipoko dancer had gotten too drunk to perform his duties properly. Consequently, the day "had lost its joy". Since the event had not been consecrated to the dead, they had not come to dance among the living. By dancing the *Lukongo*, Nzambi had recalled to the village its purpose in dancing the masks in the first place: thanksgiving for the harvests and children of the past year.

In the late 1980s, older men and women among the Eastern Pende insisted that the dead (*vumbi*) dance among the living on these occasions in a true reunion of the extended family. Pende masquerades always take place during the day, but on the eve, the talking drums boom with the rhythms for the different masks. This night-time rehearsal gives younger dancers a chance to show their mettle and alerts the countryside to the festivities. Most importantly, the drums invite the guests of honour, the village's deceased family members (who would not normally travel abroad during the heat of the day). On each day of the masquerade, the first performer must dance at one of the village altars in order to consecrate the dance to the dead. According to Nzambi, omitting this step (as happened at Kingange), was like writing a letter and then forgetting to send it. On the last day, the ill kneel before Kipoko who dances, throwing a semi-circular kick over each petitioner as a prayer requesting that the ancestors heal the petitioner and "cover" him or her with a shell of protection. Finally, one of the masks will oversee a sacrificial meal behind the chief's house for the lineage heads to honour the dead, to assure them that they have not been forgotten.

Masks are matchless in their ability to transform the most banal of public spaces into an oneiric world outside of time, where the normal rules no longer apply. There is no need to build a cathedral, manipulate the light effects, and hush everyone to silence, to create an otherworldly experience. Bring in the masks and suddenly the village square [fig. 4], a clearing in the bush [frontispiece], or Santa Monica Boulevard become sacral spaces, strange in their unfamiliarity. During the *mukanda* season, sunny, well-trodden paths become tinged by menace when audience members suddenly discern a stealthy step or rustle. Surely, there can be no better example for the uncanniness of masquerade than this estrangement of domestic spaces, the "sliding of coziness into dread" (Vidler 1992: 57).

During the village masquerades, the organisers rip public space out of the real world in order to suggest an invisible world to which the living often can be oblivious. As one man reprimanded some young graduates, who were horsing around during the refurbishment of an altar: "You're joking but you don't realise that all the dead are here, even all of the deceased [former chiefs]". Older practitioners described how, when everything had been prepared correctly, when disputes in the community were settled, when the dead were invited as they should be, when the audience participated with a full heart, the moment would come when one could sense the invisible dead dancing alongside. Here the masks most definitely *do not* represent the dead, they *do not* embody the dead (although that is what you tell children), but they create an ambience in which the sensitive viewer experiences the eerie sensation of invisible beings manifesting in the sunshine of the village square. Unexpectedly, this encounter (carefully structured both temporally and spatially) produces not dread, but joy.

DEAD EYES, HOT BODY

On both sides of the Loange River, the mask that expresses most clearly the link to the realm of the dead is Kiwoyo (Eastern Pende) or Giwoyo (Central Pende). Universally described as one of the very oldest masks, Giwoyo's headdress comprises a face with a long, tapering projection extending beyond the chin. Since this object is invariably photographed vertically, Europeans   Pl. 5, 10
have tended to interpret the projection as a beard, perhaps influenced by paintings of God the Father. In my experience, this suggestion never failed to astound Pende spectators, particularly since it fails to account for the unique manner in which this mask is worn by the performer—perched on top of his head like a baseball cap. Although the headpiece and cloth covering the mouth are sewn tightly to the costume, due to its length, the headpiece tends to flop up and down during the dance if left unsecured in the front. Consequently, sculptors drill a small hole in the middle of the projection so that a cord can be drawn through it. The dancer will hold the cord tightly   Pl. 10
between his teeth to stabilise the mask when he performs. Since the headpiece sits on top of the head, the audience seldom views it frontally in performance as they would a face mask. Instead, it is designed to be viewed in profile, with the performer's eyes obscured from view by a long raffia fringe.

The sculptor Mashini Gitshiola, schooled by his father Gitshiola Shimuna, trained in turn by the celebrated sculptor Gabama a Gingungu, offered the following interpretation: "This Giwoyo shows a cadaver in the coffin.   Pl. 10
The [projection] shows the body of the person in the coffin. The sheets are put over the cadaver. The lines cut [around the jaw line show how] when

someone dies, his face stays outside, all the body is covered". Mashini argues that the headpiece (*viewed in profile*) represents a cadaver on its funeral bier at a wake. If possible, Pende like to wait one or two nights before they bury their dead. The women wash the body, lay it out, and cover it with a sheet, pulled up to the chin. For better viewing of the body, they once propped up either the head or the entire torso with pillows of rolled cloth and left the eyes half-open.

Mashini's interpretation is unexpected but visually compelling. The depiction of a cadaver explains the half-open eyes with their unfocused stare. Truly, as Mashini described it, "eyes like that show a cadaver". The manner of propping up the head of the corpse for viewing also explains the obtuse angle at which the face of the mask is joined to the projection in most older works. The elegant abstraction of the body explains the tapering form of the projection, which reflects how the arms are placed alongside the body (under the sheet). The projection narrows as it approaches the feet and often curves up at the end as feet would. The alternating light and dark pattern (*kaji-kaji*) on the "sheet" also is used to decorate the chief's ritual house and other objects where there is a crossing of the worlds of the living and the dead.

Mashini's interpretation suggests an explanation for another extremely unusual feature of Giwoyo's presentation. The celebrated village masks appear in the public square; Giwoyo is again unique in performing entirely in the bush. It appears as twilight approaches in the grass on the fringes of the village. Part of the audience's experience of Giwoyo entails craning the neck to discern his approach through the long grass. The crowd naturally hushes as it strains to see what is happening. In the late 1980s, many Pende still believed that the spirits of the dead lingered in the bush on the borders of the village. Someone who wishes to contact a deceased relative need only go to a tree on the fringes of the village to direct his or her prayer. It is the voices of the dead that one hears distantly in the wind that sweeps across the high grass. Giwoyo dances in this realm and it is possible that its performance represents a survival of an archaic ritual in which the masquerade ushered the spirits of the departed out of the village (Strother 1998: 180).

Historian Bengo Meya-Lubu also (independently) interpreted the Central Pende Muyombo mask as representing a cadaver laid out for viewing. In plate 11, the sculptor has given riveting expression to the face of death by rendering both eyes and mouth agape. What is so masterful is how the sculptor contrasts robust sculptural volumes (forehead and cheekbones) to the flaccid organs of expression. He has miniaturised the projection but retained the sharply obtuse angle at which the head is propped up from the body. While Giwoyo's long projection makes it difficult for the performer to wear for long period, Muyombo shortens the projection to allow for more strenuous and varied performances. Also, it sits on the head quite differently. A soft hat (*tumba*) provides a secure mounting for the smaller headpiece, which now angles down the forehead.   *Pl. 11, 12, 13*

If Giwoyo's performance is associated with mystery and wonder, Muyombo calls forth ululations of joy (*miyeye*). Muyombo's signature dance includes bursts of "hot" or fast-paced, alternating footwork, high on the toes. Known for long performances on centre stage, the performer also pantomimes women's food-producing activities (hoeing, fishing, cooking, etc.). When Muyombo honours their work, the women in the audience explode in applause and show their appreciation by throwing ears of corn, calabashes, and money onto the dance-floor as praise-gifts.

Given the explanations for Giwoyo and Muyombo, one wonders if the angle of the mask slanting down the forehead was originally intended to mimic the angle at which the head is propped up from the body for viewings at wakes. Most of the oldest masks collected among the Central Pende   *Pl. 14* were worn in this fashion. Viewed in profile as they were intended, such   *Pl. 11-13, 15, 17* works present "the impressive image of a mortuary mask: the lowered eyelid… under which the dead eye can be seen" (Olbrechts [1946] 1982: 34). However, there is a delicious irony in the fact that such forehead masks always depict male faces and are associated with "hot" explosions of dance capable of galvanising an audience. Because the performer can see and breathe normally, he may run and leap freely and maintain longer outbursts of high-aerobic activity.

Pende dance criticism contrasts the "heat" of life with the coolness of death. As a familiar proverb puts it: "We came to warm ourselves in the sun's rays, [but] our home is in *kalunga* [the other-world]". Muhenge Mutala, initiated ca. 1921, explained that the masquerade is capable of "making rejoice the bodies that are shivering". The cold, the aging, and the ill assume many of the same postures as they stiffen and curl up into themselves. This withdrawal is as much psychological as physical. According to Muhenge, dance warms the body and drives out the chill of incipient death. It stimulates the weak and ill so that they feel stronger and interested in others as well as themselves. When the masquerade catches fire, the excitement becomes contagious. At such moments, both Central and Eastern Pende like to point to arthritic and elderly audience members who dance one-on-one with the masks, their aches forgotten, as they regain the heat and flexibility of youth [fig. 4].

There is good evidence that masquerades among the Central and Kwilu Pende once fulfilled the same ritual functions still respected among the Eastern Pende in 2006. Nonetheless, although the dead no longer receive prayers or sacrifices among the Central Pende, field associates insisted in the late 1980s that masquerades "strengthen the community" (*gukolesa dimbo*), "make it beautiful" (*gubongesa dimbo*), and "make it rejoice" (*gusuanguluisa dimbo*). Although secularised, the masquerade is still associated with peace and celebration and may not be performed if there are quarrels in the community.

Physiognomy of Masks

Among the Pende, it is the performers who invent masks (Strother 1998). Once young men have created a new character and worked out its dance with a professional drummer, they will consult a master sculptor who is able to create a face in harmony with the persona of the mask. Connoisseurs insist that one should be able to *see* the dance in the face. Some knowledge of Pende theories of physiognomy and gender are necessary to comprehend what this might mean.

Charles Darwin cogently defined physiognomy in 1873 as "the recognition of character through the study of the permanent form of the features". Since it focuses on bony structure (forehead, nose, chin, and cheekbones), it is quite distinct from the study of expression, which concentrates on the mobile muscles of the face. Physiognomy has a long history around the world. In Europe, the term has become problematic because of its association in nineteenth-century practice with theories of social evolution. Some physiognomists attempted to develop a system whereby all of society, indeed all of humanity, could be assigned a precise slot on a sliding scale from the human to the animal. Embedded within this system were deeply racist, classist, and sexist assumptions. However, most theatrical traditions rely on theories of physiognomy to interpret characters for their audiences and one must not project nineteenth-century European hierarchies onto other systems.

Pende physiognomy is rooted in the belief that gender is the most salient determinant of inner character. The feminine is idealised as peaceful, self-controlled and socially responsible. In contrast, men are hot, creative, energetic, emotional, prone to brooding and anger. Whereas the feminine is stable and essentialised, Central Pende sculptors outlined an entire spectrum of gendered masculinity. The average male is presumed to have the capacity for aggression but usually succeeds in funnelling that extra energy and "heat" into various physical or intellectual projects. However, the ideal man is a mediator, who has learned to "cool" his masculine aggression with positive feminine social skills. Described as "gentle" (*doux* in Franco-Kipende slang), he is naturally soft-voiced and considerate—someone who thinks before he speaks and who does not resolve his problems through physical means. Most believe that this ideal man is rare. The topic came to the fore in the late 1980s during the election of new chiefs. Many people were concerned to find a candidate "with the face of a woman", by which they meant a peacemaker (*mukandji wa athu*, a term appropriate for someone who breaks apart two fighters). After long discussions of the candidates' character, there often was a sense that one had to make do, because so few men lived up to this ideal. At the other end of the spectrum, one finds risk-takers who have the capacity for extreme physical and psychic violence. One must be careful to insist that there is no Western progress narrative of good to evil implied in the spectrum of feminine to masculine (or vice versa). Most Pende believe that all of these personalities are indispensable to the survival of society, including the inconvenient hyper-male. In their view, the man capable of burgling houses is likely to be the same man who can face down a leopard or shine in battle.

Many insist that the sexes have distinctly different personalities and that this is reflected in what they perceive to be distinctly different faces. Gendered physiognomy is most easily read in the treatment of the forehead. Any child will tell you that the feminine forehead is smooth and flat , whereas the masculine forehead is "bulging" and "lumpy". In the words of the sculptor Nguedia Gambembo: "The foreheads of men are lumpy; it shows that men are dangerous, quarrelsome, and mean. The foreheads of women are smooth and level". In plates 23-24, one can see how carvers have rendered the female forehead smooth, vertical, with only a gentle swelling. In contrast, the male forehead protrudes forcefully outwards. Forensic anthropologists claim more than 85 percent accuracy in sexing skulls for which one of their most reliable indicators is the pronounced ridge over the eye socket of the male skull (called a supraorbital torus). To increase visual legibility over the distance of the dance floor, it seems that Pende carvers have transformed the supraorbital torus into a bulging protrusion, which can be gauged to judge the degree of masculinity. There is a parallel drawn between the volumes of the face and the body language of the dance. Female characters perform on one spot with relatively contained gestures. Male masks usually keep moving and periodically burst forth in displays of propulsive energy.

The gaze is second in importance only to the forehead as an indicator of gender. In the words of Nguedia: "Men's eyes are open; they show that the individual can take care of himself, is alert and on his toes, able to solve his own problems". As illustration, he cited the case of a man who knew the law and refused to pay extortion. Open eyes are a sign simultaneously of intelligence, self-confidence and guts. He insisted that these were indubitably masculine qualities; women's eyes should be lowered to show beauty.

Although the qualities Nguedia listed are admired, "open eyes" (*meso a gualeluga*) are regarded with deep ambivalence. Most commonly described as "dangerous eyes" or even "mean eyes" (*meso abala*), they are considered predatory since they are associated with individuals who seek to control and watch over others. Open, staring eyes are the means of imposing one's own will. Therefore, in visual representation, wide-open eyes are associated with the possibility of violence. In masks, white-rimmed eyes give fair warning: "Get out of here!" [figs. 2, 5]. They usually indicate the presence of whips and the fact that these masqueraders have licence to strike if someone breaks the rules.

In contrast, men insist that a woman's gaze is naturally *zanze* (with eyes half-closed so that she looks out from slits). Many sculptors spoke of the seductive power of the *zanze* gaze. According to Nguedia Gambembo: "The hooded eyes of a woman weaken a man. Everything that she asks of you, you do without speaking, you give to her". As several Pende told the story in 1989: Adam knew that he wasn't supposed to eat the apple. He knew right from wrong. But what happened? Eve looked at him *zanze*....

Since many men speak of how alluring they find this gaze, one is tempted to translate *zanze* as "bedroom eyes", such as Marilyn Monroe and Marlene Dietrich made famous. However, there is a twist. *Zanze* is a genuinely active posture because it is rooted in an act of generosity: *I will allow you to look at* me. In contrast, "open eyes" betray an inability to discipline oneself. Generosity is the highest of Pende virtues and part of what makes *zanze* so irresistible is that it puts the viewer at ease.

Whatever the theories of physiognomy, the rules of decorum forbid men from staring (or showing the whites of their eyes) in public. They, too, must adopt the demeanour of generosity. This creates quite a challenge for sculptors of face masks, so much so that the ability to convey gender differences in the eyes is the single quality that distinguishes the work of the most highly acclaimed artists. Masculine eyes are rendered proportionately larger in the face, usually with a larger eye opening. The upper eyelid projects farther into space, thereby creating the impression of a more "open" and aggressive gaze. In plate 20, the carver rendered the upper eyelids as triangles, thrusting outwards, pulled towards the side (towards the mandibular angle). In plate 20, the carver has thickened the upper lid until it asserts as much sculptural volume as the forehead or nose. It also is pulled slightly to the side. In contrast, the feminine eyes represented in plates 23

Pl. 20, 21

Pl. 23, 24

and 24 are proportionately smaller in relation to the face. The upper eyelid is rounded and pulled downward, rather than out to the side, thereby enhancing the sense that the gaze is hooded.

More generally, the facial plane is much shallower in the feminine representation, the features much less assertive. The face is oval and softly modulated. In plates 23 and 24, the artists have chosen curving bands of cicatrices to enhance the soft plumpness in the cheeks. Stylistically, greater aggression is marked on the male representations by acute articulations in the facial features in everything from the receding hairline to the treatment of the nose. In plate 21, the sculptor has used his knife to excavate deeply the brow and sharply chisel the cheekbones. The female mouth is relatively horizontal, reflecting the belief that the more peaceable the emotions, the flatter the upper lip. In contrast the mouth of Pumbu, the killer or executioner, is large in scale and much more angular. Nguedia characterised Pumbu's mouth as "pouting", which shows that he is a "man perpetually angry, a dangerous person".

During the twentieth century, Central Pende sculptor Gabama a Gingungu (1890s-1965) became renowned for his abilities to express the full range of gendered personalities (Strother 1999). For example, his chief's mask (registered in 1932) is indisputably masculine when compared with female masks. The bulging forehead and cheeks create a distinctly peanut-shaped silhouette. The eyes are proportionately larger and wider. The brow is far more emphatic. There is a more acute transition in the cheekbones.

However, if the chief's mask is contrasted with that of Pumbu, one can easily perceive the degree to which Gabama modulated its form. Its surface is burnished and smooth. The chief's brow is broader and shallower in relief. The eyes are smaller in size and the eyelids "drop"; they are not pulled to the side as they are in plates 20 and 21. In profile, the horns of the coiffure are blunter and the nose and chin are rounded. The sculptor Zangela Matangua particularly admired the subtlety of Gabama's handling of the mouth with its relatively flattened upper lip: "A man's mouth rises up, but his is lowered a little, because his face shows coolness like the face of a woman".

In sum, what Pende connoisseurs admire in Gabama's chief's mask is his ability to render concrete the abstraction of the chief "with the female face". He portrays the chief as a man who is unquestionably male, potent, the father of many children, who nonetheless commands feminine social skills. The chief's mask was invented in the 1910s and spread quickly over a wide territory. In contrast to the negative reality of what the chief had become during the colonial period, the mask asserted *what he ought to be*. During a period of intense censorship, masqueraders found a means to criticise the power-mad. The mask's popularity reasserted a counter-image, a counter-model, of the "chief with the face of a woman" during a period of oppression.

One of the most easily recognisable of Central Pende masks is the black-and-white Mbangu. The example collected by Emil Torday in 1909 is a forehead mask (without eye openings). The face is divided into black-and-white, but otherwise is identical to Pota, Ginjinga, or any number of male masquerades known for "hot", virile dances. As future dancers reinvented Mbangu as a true face mask, sculptors became interested in expressing the complexity of Mbangu's condition. One sculpture from the 1950s represents a high point in Central Pende art history in which the artist capitalises on the interpretive possibilities of Pende physiognomic theory.

Mbangu dances to the song, "We look on (unable to help), the sorcerers have bewitched him". The masker wears a humpback from which an arrow extends [fig. 9]. The arrow refers to the folklore on sorcerers "shooting" their prey with invisible arrows when they cast their spell. The metaphor communicates the perception of sudden onslaught in illness or misfortune. We say, "It came out of the blue". Mbangu advances, lunging down on one knee, and then the other. The master dancer Khoshi Mahumbu interprets this gesture as feints intended to dodge the arrows of his assailant. Mbangu sometimes performs with a bow and arrows himself, aiming at random, thereby conveying his wish to strike back at the source of his misfortune and his frustration at not knowing where to look. Under his costume, Mbangu wears the wooden bells carried by hunting dogs. Their distinctive hollow sound accentuates the feints of his dance and recalls the life-and-death struggle taking place. Mbangu is both hunted and hunter as he searches for the man who disabled him. Mbangu is "bewitched"; however, since the Pende worldview attributes almost all illness and personal misfortune to the malice of others, what really is at issue is chronic illness or disability and our response to it.

Beginning with Jean vanden Bossche, there has been a tendency to describe masquerade characters as "types" (1950). De Sousberghe categorised Mbangu as "the epileptic" (1959: 43; 1960b: 523). However, this is far too specific. In fact, more often than not, masquerade figures are complex composites, of which Mbangu is a particularly good example. The black-and-white division of Mbangu's face evokes the scars of someone who fell into the fire (Ndambi 1975: 126, 128) due to epilepsy or some other medical condition. Scientists have demonstrated that the flickering flames of night-time campfires are proven triggers for seizures. However, the scars associated with epilepsy are only one of Mbangu's symptoms. He wears a humpback. If he does not carry a bow and arrows, dancers usually avail themselves of a cane to indicate his general physical weakness. Many sculptors depict the traces of smallpox on the black eyelid, and the face distorted by a paralysis of the facial nerve. The multiplication of complaints signals that Mbangu does not represent any one illness. Instead, the sculptor and performer collaborate to make Mbangu a composite sign for illness and disability, of all the misfortunes that might befall someone.

The black-and-white coloration deserves further comment. Colour symbolism in the masks is usually positional. While white can have several meanings, the most common one comes through its association with the white kaolin clay used in all healing rites. On the other hand, black is the shade of sorcery and illness and it is striking that all the marks of deformation fall on the black side. Therefore, the bi-coloration depicted may have a secondary meaning in situating Mbangu at the crossroads between healing (health) and illness. Pl. 18

On the "healthy" side, Mbangu displays (according to Pende physiognomic theory) features appropriate to masculine form: assertive forehead, well-articulated cheekbones, and projecting eyes, although all but the eyes have received muted, even "feminised" expression. On the other hand, witness the distortions wreaked to Mbangu's left side. By keeping the upper line of the eyebrows level on both sides, but greatly thickening the brow on the deformed side, the sculptor achieves a masterful sense of the face being dragged downward on that side, while preserving the harmony of the whole. He has also twisted the nose and mouth to a great degree on the same side. Nonetheless, the physical deformations are only part of the story. There has been a sad transformation of character as well. On the "ill" side, the artist has undercut the brow, thereby creating the impression that it protrudes. Instead of rounding the cheekbone, he has acutely angled it. He has also sharpened the tips of the eyelid and pulled it down towards the mandibular angle. Finally, he has rendered the nose exceedingly long and razor-tipped. The reader will recognise all of these changes as belonging to the physiognomy of aggression. Facing the challenge of chronic disability, Mbangu is also facing the challenge of bitterness and envy. The artist has gone far beyond the naturalistic representation of a physical complaint to comment on the toll of chronic illness on the psyche.

What then is to be our response to Mbangu? Some sculptors render the mask comedic, but this work conveys an extraordinary delicacy by contrasting the gentle perfection of the features on one side with their systematic distortion on the other. This sculptor responds to the widespread version of Mbangu's song: "Do not mock your neighbour, Do not laugh at your brother. The sorcerers have bewitched him". In other words, anyone may fall prey to misfortune. It could happen to you.

CHIEFS AS PATRONS: TEN HEARTS HAVE I

Pende chieftaincy was once a ritual office. The chief was first and foremost a priest serving as intermediary between the living and the dead. His house is described as the "house of the dead", "the house of seed", "the house of meat", because it safeguards the portal through which the dead can send children, bountiful harvests and hunts to their junior relatives. During the colonial era, the Belgians did all they could to transform the office of chief into political officer for the state, with the result that the office has been permanently tainted among the Kwilu and Central Pende. Eastern Pende chiefs have better maintained their ritual position and, consequently, respect for their office.

Nonetheless, as history will demonstrate, not all chiefs play by the rules. In the words of Chief Kende (Katshivi a Khoji),

"The chief has many hearts. Because one day, you will be angry. On that day, you have the heart of a leopard. On that day, [your] blood has the colour red. Another day, you feel compassion, you take the colour, you have a white heart. Another day, you are malicious and [turn to] sorcery [*wanga*] because [your] heart is bad. It has the colour black. [This is why] they say that the chief has ten hearts".

Kende argued that the door of a paramount chief's house and the hem of his ceremonial skirt are both edged with alternating patterns of red, white and black so that people never forget that the chief is human. He has rivals; he hears hurtful criticism; he may crave power. Therefore, he needs to be watched like a hawk. Petitioners should be careful to call forth the compassionate side of his nature by showing appreciation for past good deeds, by recalling great chiefs in the past, and by emphasising the nurturing mandate for his office.

Pl. 8   The beloved Eastern Pende Kipoko mask reminds the chief of his higher calling. Every chief of every rank has the right to Kipoko. Typically, sculptors exaggerate the mask's eyes, nose and ears, but render the mouth diminutive or nonexistent. Thus they convey that the chief should benefit from a kind of sensory hyperactivity to know everything that is happening in his community, and yet be slow to speech lest hasty words render a bad situation worse. When asked about the mask's long nose, many field associates responded that it showed how the chief must be sensitive to the "smell of stolen meat". Frankly, I considered this explanation contrived until it was lived out before my eyes. My host, Chief Kende, returned home one day in 1987, agitated because he had smelled goat meat cooking behind a closed

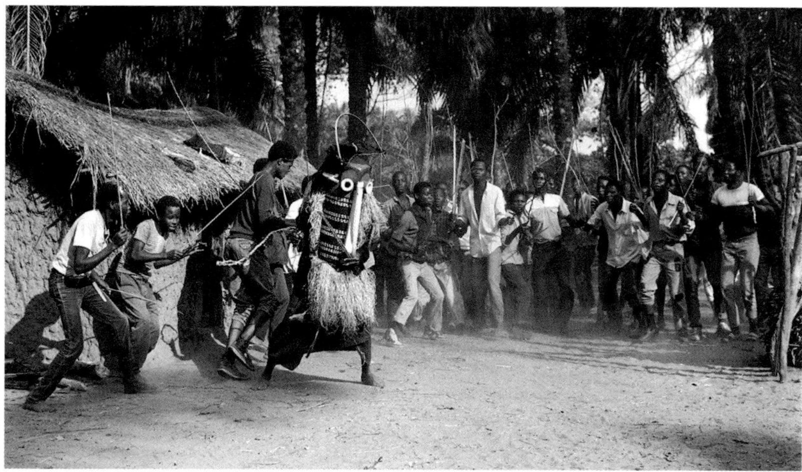

Fig. 5. The Eastern Pende version of the mask Pumbu, danced at the illness of Chief Kombo-Kiboto (Mukanzo a Kilumbu). Ndjindji, DRC, 1987. Photograph: Z. S. Strother

kitchen door. Many Pende find cooking behind closed doors suspicious since it reveals a desire to hoard. In this case, the chief knew for a fact that the villager in question owned no livestock whatsoever. When I asked what he intended to do, Kende lived out the counsel of the mask. "Nothing!" he insisted, as a chief must never voice accusations or incite quarrels. Kende waited until the owner of the goat discovered his loss and then discreetly pointed the investigation in the right direction.

If Kipoko represents all that is warm and nurturing about the chief as the guardian of his people, another mask, Pumbu [fig. 5] depicts a different chief. Reserved for only a handful of the Eastern Pende's most powerful chiefs, it dances rarely—only in the event of special problems, such as a chief's serious illness, regional epidemic, or famine. Pumbu represents the executive branch of the office, which must sometimes impose punishment for crime or endorse war. The Pende associate wide-open eyes, showing lots of white, with anger unleashed. Hence Pumbu's protruding white-rimmed eyes express an aesthetic of fear.

Pumbu dances holding a warrior's bow and arrow and flashing a sword or machete in one hand, straining against the cords that bind him to one or two young men. More young men accompany him, bearing whips, singing Pumbu's signature song: "Are you afraid?" At the climax of the dance, the masquerader whirls and cuts the cords that restrain him. The crowd flees shouting "Have pity, sir!" Whereas Kipoko ends his performance through a danced prayer for healing, Pumbu must kill a chicken or other animal to provide for an expiatory sacrifice. The two masks never meet, nor perform together. To a great extent, these two visions of chieftaincy are irreconcilable.

In his description of the chief's multiple hearts, Kende spoke of the temptation for the chief to resort to *wanga*, which are preparations used to manipulate the material and spirit world for personal advantage. The use of perfume to solicit a positive physical response from others is a commonplace use of *wanga*. The emphasis on private gain is important, because it lends the term a distinct pejorative connotation for the Pende (grown stronger through Christian evangelism) that perhaps justifies its translation as "sorcery". *Wanga* is associated with *all* talents and abilities that surpass the ordinary, but it also may be used to kill or cause illness.

The dilemma is this. The chief's most urgent duty is to protect his people. He must make sure that the portals to the world of the dead remain open and unpolluted so that the ancestors can communicate with their junior relatives and he also must guard against those who foment discord through theft, adultery, false witness, etc. Since some individuals seek to do harm through knowledge of *wanga*, he must understand how it works in order to neutralise it or to intimidate potential malefactors from putting their schemes into motion. *However, if he knows* wanga, *how to prevent him from sometimes using it for his own personal ends?*

Fears about the misuse of *wanga* become acute in the reception of sculptures surrounding the ritual house (*kibulu* or *gisendu*) for the chieftaincy. According to a favourite story in Ndjindji, Chiefs Kombo-Kiboto and Maï-Munene had the custom of exchanging gifts of cloth at funerals. But one day things changed. Some say that a young and ambitious Kombo began to resent exchanging gifts and wished to establish his superiority over Maï. Some place the blame on Maï and say that he began to demand tribute from Kombo. In any case, Kombo bided his time until his youth had matured and he had a good number of men to arm. He then rebuilt his ritual house and mounted a statue on the roof (*kishikishi*) in female form, which he named "Katshina". Maï's wife was named Katshina and Maï interpreted this gesture both as a death threat targeting his wife (who hailed from Kombo's town) and as an act of war. He attacked Kombo, who eventually prevailed, but at the cost of considerable loss of life.

Many *mukanda* songs deride the ambition of chiefs. In this cautionary tale on how leaders can trick their people into war, Kombo cleverly found the means to manipulate both the living and the dead. If Maï attacked, Kombo's people would have no recourse but to fight back. Similarly, "war [demands] a curse" (*Ita, mukumbu*). The chief must vocalise his grounds for waging war in a public speech during which he appeals to the collective dead to punish his enemies. If he does not, he is sure to lose, because he will be fighting alone. Many Pende assured me that the dead weigh the truthfulness of such speeches; they will not support acts of naked aggression. By provoking Maï to attack, Kombo sought to secure just cause for himself. His pyrrhic victory demonstrated that the dead were not so easily hoodwinked.

In a fierce competition for prestige, a handful of great chiefs won the right to display large anthropomorphic figures on the roof and surround their doors with panels carved in relief. Some in Ndjindji cite Kombo's struggle with Maï as the origin for this practice. Whether or not this is true, the story communicates apprehension regarding the chief's use of *wanga*. Did Kombo mount the statue to protect the community *or* further his own ambition?

Pl. 35-37

It is the relative naturalism of such works that sparks anxiety. All figurative sculpture is reserved for the chief; however, sculptors were adamant, unanimous, that masks *do not* represent ("resemble") living human beings. Masks number among the *mahamba*, tools for contacting the collective dead. Other altar sculptures may depict a face or upper torso, but the handling of the body will be deliberately schematic. Fully-modelled three-dimensional sculpture is rarely acceptable for use as *mahamba*.

Instead, figurative sculptures are portrayed as "workers" and widely associated with the practice of *wanga* since their naturalistic language raises the question of individual models. The very question of portraiture makes sculptors visibly nervous. When Kombo mounted the *kishikishi*, he was playing on such fears to say that he had authorised the taking of one or more human lives through sorcery in order to "strengthen" or "reinforce" (*kukolesa*) the chiefdom. The chief is allowed a certain number of power objects to protect himself and his people. The *kishikishi* perches on the centre post of the house [fig. 6] and watches over the community. It communicates the warning: this chief is protected by spirit sentinels, who never have cause to sleep or even blink. Should you attempt evil, he has the ability to identify and punish. Although the form for these objects has varied significantly over the twentieth century, many patrons have preferred female imagery, emphasising the fiercely protective nature of the chief through association with idealised feminine behaviour.

Usually, chiefs maintain deniability. They must carefully preserve their image as nurturers. The naturalism alludes to a human model without being precise enough to identify a particular individual. Did he or didn't he? Since rumours flourish wherever secrecy is practised, fears about the

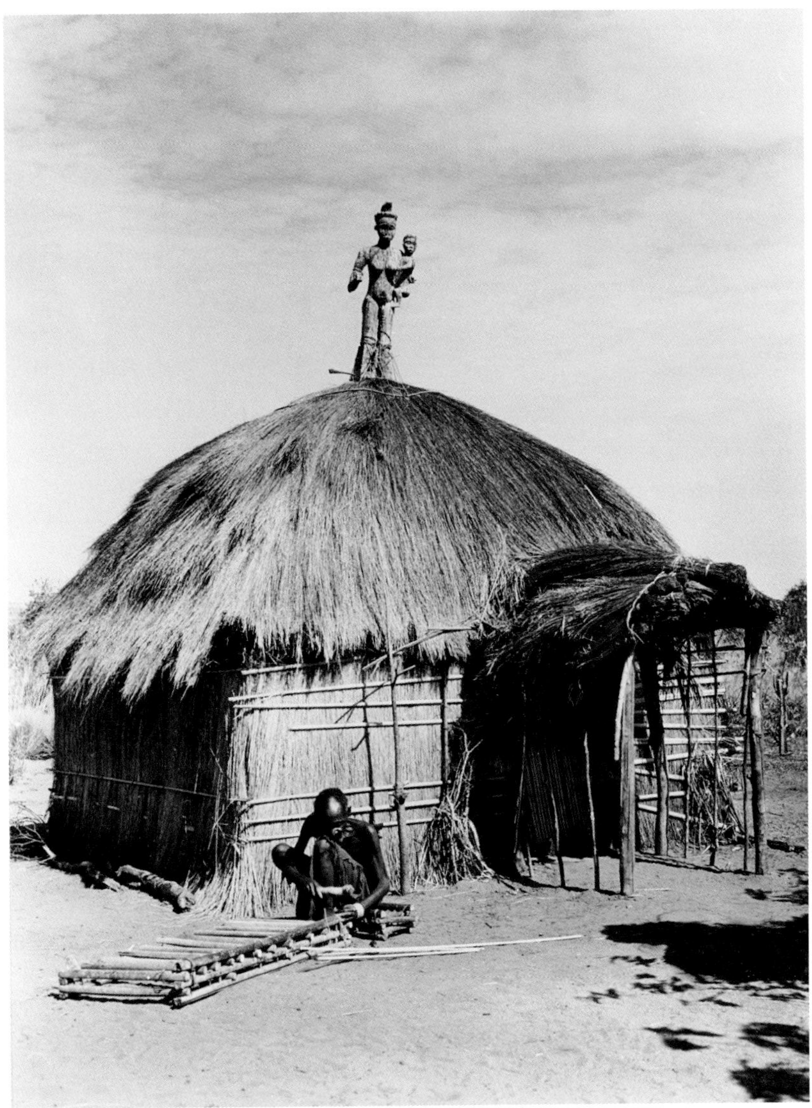

Fig. 6. The *kibulu* (ritual house) of Chief Komba ornamented with a rooftop finial
sculpted by Kaseya Tambwe, ca. 1947. Photo: C. Lamote, 1950s, InforCongo
no. 31.226/27. Royal Museum for Central Africa, Tervuren, photo EPH 3003

significance of mounting such works are confirmed in any of the routine
deaths that occur in the months before or after the placement of the figures.
In the story, what was so shocking was that Kombo took responsibility and
actually gave the statue a personal name, the name of his niece. Thereby,
he left no doubt that the sculpture was a portrait and that he intended to
capture Katshina's spirit to work for him.

Who's Looking at Whom?

The chief's house is surrounded by an army of eyes designed to trigger the uneasy sensation of being stared at (Strother 2004a: 286-89). The faces marked on the chief's ritual furniture, altars, and architectural sculpture are intended to communicate a warning to those approaching to weigh the consequences of proximity. Do they have permission to be there? What are their motives? Pende speakers commonly evoke the gaze when interpreting these works. Some described the figures as "looking at" the courtyard, house, or chief (drawing on the verb *kutala*). Many others used the verb *kubamba*, which signifies "to protect" in the sense of "to watch over". For example, *kubamba* is the verb used to describe the action of a babysitter watching over a child. It connotes vigilance due to the implication that the object of concern is vulnerable, requiring the agent to pay attention.

One stool dramatically captures the gazes radiating outwards from the person of the chief. A large female figure bears the weight of the sitter while two small, male figures look out in opposite directions. The stool warns that the chief has the means to know what is happening in every direction. His spirit sentinels are vigilant. Even the female figure's gaze is activated. Although her eyes are lowered, their upper lids protrude far enough into space to create shadows. One of the little figures has wide staring eyes (like the masks who carry whips) and tightly grips a medicated horn close to his stomach.

Usually caryatid stools from Central Africa offer a vision of stability and quiet containment, but this artist defies convention. One could hardly imagine a more energised composition than this one. The two male figures shoot off at diagonals from the central figure. Fearlessly, the sculptor has dislocated the limbs from the central torso and reconfigured them as a free-floating "drawing in wood", to borrow a phrase from William Rubin, who observed that the best Pende sculptures are often remarkable for "the way in which intense mass and surface drawing are made to cohabit" (1987: 58-60). The dynamism of the zigzagging lines framing the figure imbues the work with vitality.

Marking the chief's stool was also intended to serve as a warning to others. In 1988, whenever Chief Nzambi would take leave following a visit, he would stand behind his chair and incline it forward. I observed this gesture as a personal eccentricity. However, it transpired later that adults frequently warn children not to touch the chief's possessions: "A chief walks with his *mahamba*". Because he lives in a house intended to serve as the portal to the other world, and because he communicates regularly with the dead through special altars (*mahamba*), spirits may be drawn to him and pose a danger to others. Nzambi tipped his chair as a means to dislodge any spirits who might

Pl. 33-37

Pl. 34

have alighted nearby. "Time to go!" He explained that such gestures used to be unnecessary because chiefs had sculpted stools or chairs, which no one outside their families dared touch.

Pl. 35   An early roof finial (collected before 1911) demonstrates the same compositional strategy as the stool in organizing figures gazing outward from a central axis. In 1905, Leo Frobenius documented three other finials among the Eastern Pende, which all featured a large figure raised above two to four smaller figures, all gazing in different directions (1988: figs. 376-78). From any angle, visitors approaching the chief's house become aware that they are the focus of many eyes.

However, the gaze trained on the chief is not wholly protective of his person; it is also wary and suspicious of his motives. At a large public meeting in 1987, one speaker asserted that the figures kept within the chief's house have a twofold purpose: "If someone is impudent, they will pursue the malefactors. If the chief himself disobeys the laws, he will die. His own guard can kill him". The surprising conclusion of the meeting was that the guards placed in the back room of the ritual house protect the chiefdom *from the chief* as much as from outside assault!

Ironically, neither the chief nor his wife may enter the back room of their own house, where the sculptures are kept. In fact, some believe that they might well die if they catch a glimpse of certain forbidden objects within (Kodi 1976 vol. 2: 127). The only individual allowed inside is the "minister of the chamber", appointed by the chief's maternal uncles. Inside this room, the minister is presumed to maintain power objects designed to protect the chief, to serve as mystical bodyguards. In 1988, at Ndjindji, these took the form of
Pl. 39, 40, 42   a miniature leopard and boa constrictor (Strother 2004a: 290). In the past, some families commissioned fine sculptures from recognised artists.

Although visitors might see the sculptor carving such a statuette, once it was consecrated, it disappeared into the shadowy realm of the forbidden chamber, viewed only in the imagination of the community. Nonetheless, the patina on such works is often witness to loving care on the part of the
Pl. 39, 40   work's guardian. The patrons of plates 39 and 40 preferred to commission supple female forms, drawing on the belief that women demonstrate greater gifts for obedience and concentration. Although the Eastern Pende sculptor is careful to evoke the alluring feminine gaze, the shape of the head recalls
Pl. 8   the helmet mask of Kipoko and is covered with the design reserved to mark all possessions by the chief.

Some of the anxieties about chiefs' illicit acquisition of mystical knowledge are expressed in stories about their ability to shift shape. One extraordinary
Pl. 27   sculpture seems to manifest this belief quite explicitly. Its size, degree of

naturalism and heavy wood indicate that it must have been made for the inner chamber of the chief's house and the blue paint used in the rider's shirt suggests a mid-twentieth-century date. It depicts a man riding a horned animal. Herbert Cole has compared it to the sculptures from far distant Songo in central Angola, which incorporated imagery of traders riding oxen (1989: 131). However, the carvings from Songo almost always depict reins and (upturned) naturalistic horns (Bastin 1994: figs. 178, 180-83).

Although Lt. Mueller of the Wissmann expedition records travelling on a "riding ox" among the Eastern Pende (Wissmann 1974 [1888]: 107), it seems more likely that the figure represents the chief metamorphosing into a bush buffalo (*Pagasa*), one of the most feared of his familiars. Heavy, fast, aggressive, the bush buffalo (a subspecies of the widely ranging *Syncerus caffer*—commonly known as the Cape buffalo) was once responsible for more hunters' deaths than any other animal. The wounded buffalo also has the reputation for being both cunning and vengeful and its association with the chief spoke to his jealous policing of rank and its privileges. The deep eye-sockets, tapered face, and prominent nostrils are consistent with many representations of *Pagasa* in Central Pende masquerading. The depiction of horns is never naturalistic. In this case, the artist has rotated the horns backwards and down in order to enhance the fusion of rider and beast. Instead of using reins, the rider leans forward and rests his weight directly on the horns, a gesture that also emphasises his complete control over the potentially unruly force below. This representation is more iconic and less anecdotal than that found in Songo sculptures. The artist has increased the volume and mass of the rider to the point where, from a frontal view, one could mistake the legs of the buffalo for the legs of the figure. The rider's head (with coiffure) is equivalent in size to that of the buffalo, and his bulging biceps, tight grip, and out-thrust chest all convey virile mastery.

To a remarkable degree, the artist has transferred the conventions for representing the chief in twentieth-century Central Pende masquerading to sculpture. Masculine characteristics include the ridged, protruding forehead (accentuated by the placement of brass tacks), sharply angled cheekbones, and razor-sharp points of the receding hairline. However, the aggressive qualities of the representation are all softened: the face is wide, part of the forehead flattened, and the horns of his coiffure are broad and blunt. Most strikingly, the half-open, hooded eyes capture the feminine gaze *zanze*. Even in such a virile representation, the artist has been careful to evoke the chief "with the face of a woman", whose actions are tempered by compassion.

The most extraordinary of the sculptures commissioned for the chief's ritual house depicts Maximilien Balot, the Belgian officer killed during the   Pl. 42

Pende Rebellion in 1931. Without the work's collection history, it would be easy to mistake it for a "colon", a West African carving of Europeans fashioned for the tourist market. The work is unique in the Pende corpus for its close attention to the officer's uniform, its lapels, buttons, belt and shoes. The rigid body language of the sculpture contrasts strongly with that used for most Pende sculpture. For example, whereas the female sculptures have flexed knees and crooked arms, the Belgian officer stands ram-rod straight with locked knees and straight arms held tightly to his side. Although the carver has depicted the figure according to conventions of European sculpture, the work conforms nonetheless to norms of Pende representation for an angry, mercilesss physiognomy. The face is long and narrow, with protruding forehead. The eyes are wide-open and their crisp framing emphasises how much the whites of the eyes would be visible. Truly, these are "dangerous eyes" (*meso abala*). In desperate times, this figure testifies to a desire for the chief to be able to usurp the power of the colonial state in order to protect his community.

Judicial Staffs: Exceptions that Prove the Rule

Among the Kwilu Pende, *ngambi* (sometimes translated as "judges" or "orators") developed unusual prestige and were able to establish an exceptional claim on figural sculpture in the form of ceremonial staffs. During the first half of the twentieth century, clans facing serious problems would consult *ngambi*, professional advocates, who could advise their clients on the likelihood of winning a case and the costs risked. They would represent the clan in negotiations behind closed doors or (if the worst prevailed) in public trials. At the trial, the orator often was likened to a "dancer" (*mulumbu*) who began his speech by saying "I have come to dance before you" (de Sousberghe 1961: 11). To mark the seriousness of the occasion, each clan brought their family's ceremonial staff and arrows, which the orators would use during their performance, to accentuate important arguments. The cane would pass among the advocates speaking for a given family. Each would plead the clan's position, while gripping the pommel of the staff. As de Sousberghe describes it, from 1951-53, "songs and speeches [at trials] were danced, the orator punctuating his speech with moments when he raced towards the opposing party, or from one party to the other, [these] dashes ending in half-turns, when he [spun and] drove [either] his arrows or the judicial staff [*muhango*] into the ground" (1961: 11). At the end, the canes were planted before the presiding judge until the sentence was announced the following day. At that time, the winner's staff would be anointed with kaolin (de Sousberghe 1959: 99).

De Sousberghe stressed that these staffs appeared only during the most serious disputes between clans, never individuals, when all mediation had failed. In the past, each side was required to secure their claim by bringing a certain number of hostages, who risked being enslaved if the family lost the case and was required to pay heavy fines (1959: 98-99). Because of the danger involved, the staffs were charged with medicines attached in little bundles or in packed horns or sometimes through insertions of medicated earth into the body of the cane itself (ibid.: 99), which were all intended to "guide the thoughts" of the speaker (Sikitele 1986: 127) and to make his words persuasive (de Sousberghe 1959: 21).

Even today, Pende do not underestimate the power of speech (Strother 2000). In fact, the ability to dominate is presumed to rest upon rhetorical, rather than physical, prowess. Gifted mediators are both respected and feared for their abilities to manipulate the thoughts of their audiences to the point of persuading people to do what they swore they would not. Many suspect that prominent orators seek *kiboba*, special medicines that secure domination through the voice. Therefore, it is not surprising that the *mihango* (*sing. muhango*) became targets of iconoclasm, in 1954-55, when Pende Catholic teachers reinterpreted the canes as "fetishes" and threw them in the Kwilu River (de Sousberghe 1959: 21, 106).

The beauty of Kwilu Pende staffs is therefore deceiving. One must remember that they were but rarely viewed—and on occasions when lives literally were at risk. The human form alludes to reinforcement through sorcery to secure a spirit-worker to aid the advocates pleading the family's cause. In plate 32, some of the attachments usually stripped from the canes   Pl. 32
by an earlier generation of collectors still remain. The sculptor creates a cubistic tension in which two perspectives are mapped onto a single body. First, the body is evoked in stillness in which the raised head, cylindrical neck, tight tucking of the upper arms against the body, and straight spine all reinforce the rigid vertical of the cane itself. However, the diagonal alignment of forearms, thighs and feet create a counter-rhythm. The sculptor thereby signals two different postures simultaneously: standing straight and standing with knees far forward. The graphic scoring of fingers and toes calls attention to the foremost extension of the frontal plane, which is created by bending the fingers and toes a full 90°. Moreover, the carver has stopped the forward thrust of the figure by bluntly slicing through the kneecaps with his adze. The figure is frozen and yet in motion.

The degree to which the sculptor of plate 32 has reconfigured the body according to a cerebral discipline is highlighted through contrast to another judicial staff where the sculptor invokes instead the tactile qualities of soft

Pl. 31   flesh. This exquisite finial (cut down from a full-sized cane) depicts a young woman, fully frontal and yet with a whisper of suppleness (as in the slight bend of the knees). Everything about this figure is meant to be alluring. She wears the *guhota sanga* hairstyle, with hundreds of light, rolled braids encircling the head, topped by a long inverted raffia cone (*mukombe*) (Strother 1998: 52-55). This hairstyle is appreciated because it quivers with the slightest motion and enhances the movements of the head [fig. 7]. Everything speaks of careful grooming. The delineation of the individual braids creates a tactile contrast to the smooth sheen of the surface, which in turn conveys the gloss of healthy and well-maintained skin. The forehead is high and rounded and shaped by careful plucking of the hairline. The figure's knee-length wrapper is tied tightly around the hips to accentuate the buttocks. The belt around her waist evokes *jigita*, ropes of black discs made from the earliest plastics, which bobbed on the woman's waist as she walked or danced. The crispness of the carving of this belt also draws unusual attention to the hips and recalls the beads many women wore *underneath* their wrapper as an erotic enhancement. There is an unusual specificity about this figure with its wiry arms and budding breasts that may suggest a particular well-loved body. Most strikingly, the female figure displays the most naturalistic representation possible of the feminine gaze, *zanze*; the upper eyelids of the female figure create the impression that the eyes are heavy and about to close over the recessed eyeball.

     As in the masks, knowledge of twentieth-century Pende gender theory

Pl. 32   is required to appreciate the full import of the sculptures. The taut suspension of the male figure suggests a readiness to act, an ability to process information quickly. He is alert to means to forward the interests of the family. In contrast, the seductive qualities of the female figure evoke the

Pl. 31   *kiboba* medicine, the ability of the orator to manipulate his audience, to dissolve their will and powers of discernment through honeyed speech.

     Although an outstanding orator in the family was once appointed guardian of the staff (*muhango*), the object never belonged to him personally. In fact, such Kwilu staffs numbered among the very few inheritable objects among the Pende. As clan property, the *muhango* was carved in hard wood, polished by use, and passed to another person on its keeper's death (de Sousberghe 1959: 21, 99). Following the iconoclasm of the 1950s, staffs returned to a more familiar pattern. No longer associated with judges, they have become appreciated items of chiefly regalia. In the late 1980s, Kwilu sculptors (especially from the Kandale area) were circulating widely, offering staffs to chiefs. Among the Central and Eastern Pende, these sculptures are reserved unconditionally for chiefs because of their figuration. Although they sometimes

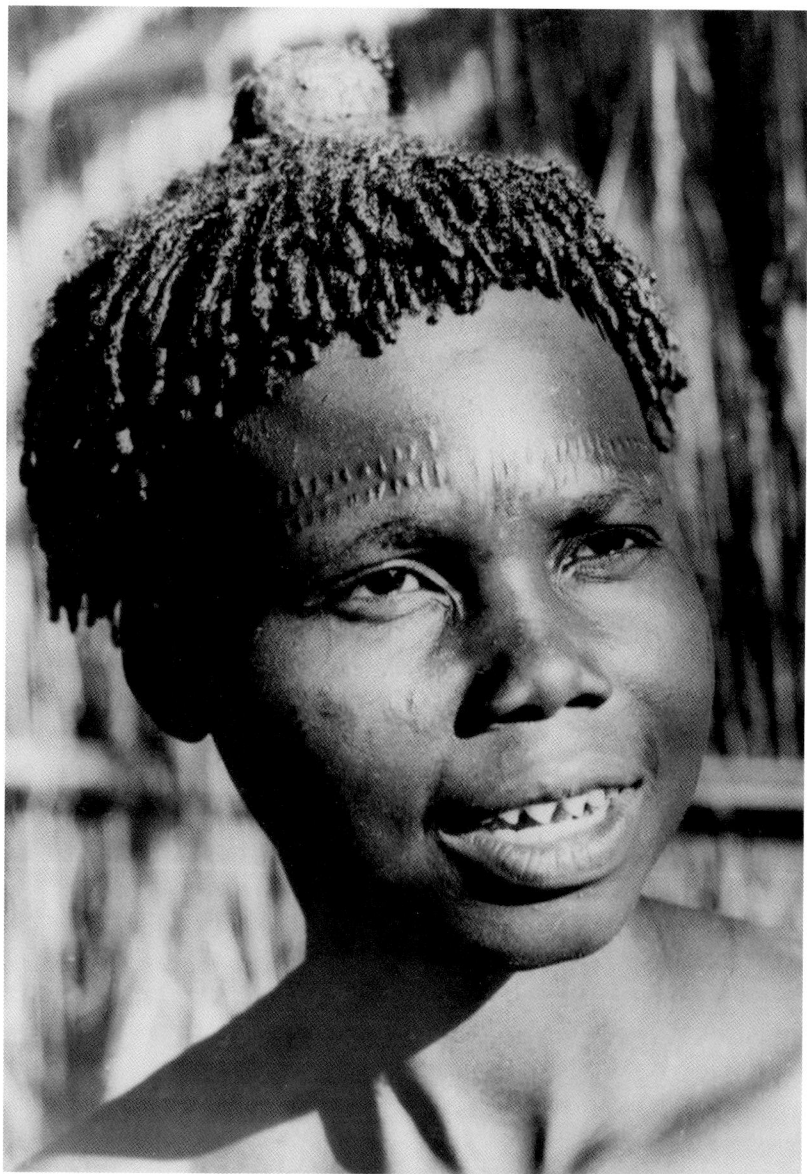

Fig. 7. Pende Woman whit the *guhota sanga* hairstyle, ca. 1950.
Photo: C. Lamote. InforCongo no. 21.652/1. Royal Museum for Central Africa,
Tervuren, photo EPH. 2968

depict a man or woman, they more often represent curling serpents or
crocodiles to show the chief's audacity (*unzui*). Notably, Mobutu Sese Seko,
longtime dictator of Zaïre, adopted one such Kwilu Pende staff, which he
displayed for many years in formal portraits.

A Colonial Encounter

The Chokwe in Angola reinvented Portuguese chairs as aesthetic objects, as frames on which to picture the realms under the beneficent supervision of the chief, including masquerading, food preparation, hunting, divination, drumming, and human reproduction. Since the high relief of the carvings was uncomfortable to lean against, chiefs seldom sat on these works, but positioned them nearby during important consultations. (Not understanding this difference, European photographers often posed individuals perched on the chairs, leaning forward to protect their backs.) In the mid-1890s, Chokwe invaded Pende country and suffered several routs by Pende and Mbuun just before the Belgian occupation. While there is no evidence that the Pende sculpted chairs in the nineteenth century, a number of carvers appropriated Chokwe models during the colonial period to fashion chairs for certain chiefs but mainly for a booming European market.

Undoubtedly the most famous of these, Muledi, worked in the village Mukulu-Nzambi on the left bank of the Kwilu until his death in 1946 (de Sousberghe 1959: 116). Muledi had studied with another respected artist, Muhungu of Ngenda (letter from Tukweso Donatien to de Sousberghe dated 8 Oct. 1958), who worked out of a community of Pende refugees living on Mbuun land (de Sousberghe 1959: 26n. 2). In this fluid frontier zone, Pende carvers enjoyed Mbuun clients, so much so that de Sousberghe describes the Mbuun town of Mukulu as a "center of Pende sculpture" (ibid.: 26). It is testimony to Muledi's reputation that Chief Gambunda paid him 200 francs and ten bolts of cloth (valued at 750 francs) to commission a chair for his investiture in 1924 (ibid.: 116). This extraordinary sum went far beyond what most sculptors received then or now (Strother 1999: 23). De Sousberghe took photographs of one of his chairs in the field in 1957 (1959: figs. 207, 208) and used the photographs to attribute another chair to Muledi from the collection of the Africa Museum in Tervuren. Another work by the same hand is in the collection of the Museum Rietberg in Zürich (Bocola 1995: 150-51). The Rietberg chair contains many scenes clearly drawn from Chokwe models. However, in other works, Muledi developed a uniquely personal interpretation of chieftaincy.

From 1913 to 1931, the colonial administration took an increasingly direct role in selecting Pende chiefs and regrouping clans and villages, actions which provoked bitter land and political disputes that continue into the present (Sikitele 1986: 323-27). By the 1920s, many chiefs had been transformed from ritual intermediaries into petty despots, whose badge of authority had become the whip. The state wished appointed chiefs (*chefs médaillés*) to accompany territorial officers for "tax" collection and execute punitive measures (flogging, seizing livestock, even burning houses) (Sikitele 1986: 694). These measures hit the Kwilu Pende particularly hard when the Huileries du Congo Belge (HCB) began to recruit workers in 1921 to produce palm oil on its plantations at Lusanga (Leverville), more than 200 kilometres from the Pende frontier. The Kwilu Pende did not have other means to pay their taxes and territorial agents pressured chiefs (with promises of premiums and under threat of flogging and arrest) to provide workers. Because the conditions at Lusanga were execrable and the pay derisory, Kwilu Pende very much resented the complicity of their chiefs in this forced labour. Oppressive HCB recruiting was the single most important factor leading to the Pende rebellion of 1931 and Muledi's own Shimuna chiefdom was one of the last to surrender.

In the Tervuren chair, Muledi indicts the collusion of economic and political interests in the colonial regime. Along one side, the artist has depicted a line of men carrying calabashes of palm oil on their shoulders, alluding to the hated forced labour assignments in which the local chiefs participated. Along another side, a white officer is travelling in a sedan chair, guarded by a file of African soldiers bearing rifles. Along the back of the chair, another officer rides a bicycle. The chair is covered by intricately carved spots and its legs end in "paws", which are set off by thick bracelets, such as chiefs often wore. Thereby, Muledi depicts the chief as a leopard. Pende despise the leopard as a "thief" who (like the tax collector) takes without giving.

The reference to leopards also underscores the threatening nature of chieftaincy during these years. Extraordinarily, the two figures and "mask" carved along the top of the chair have been equipped with glass eyes so that they reference power objects, or occult supports for power. The eyes of the central mask have even been hollowed out from the back so that light can shine through, creating an uncanny impression. These forms are unprecedented in Pende sculpture. One wonders if Muledi could have seen Kongo *minkisi* (power objects) or their reproductions. In any case, the literalness of the glassy, staring eyes, flashing white in anger, increases the sense of danger generated by the work. J. Maréchal photographed this chair before 1930 in the possession of a *chef médaillé* among the Mbuun (just across the river from Mukulu-Nzambi). The chair demonstrates this individual's identification with the power structure of the colonial regime, including forced labour and tax collection.

The bicyclist framed in the centre of the chair requires further comment. Congolese only achieved widespread access to bicycles in the 1950s. In the 1920s and 1930s, when transportation was still difficult, bicycles played a significant role in the technology of occupation. The police and the military both made widespread use of them for reconnaissance, arrests, patrols, and combat (Vanderstraeten 2001). However, it is possible that the figure represents a motorcyclist. De Sousberghe's colleague, J. de Decker, bought a chair around 1933-34, which sounds similar to the one in Tervuren; unfortunately, its location is unknown. De Decker believed that the vehicle represented a motorcycle, which was first introduced into the region by *Agent Territorial* Gaspard. He argued that the artist sought to create an impression of speed by having the figure lean forward and by stretching his legs out horizontally across the wheels (de Sousberghe 1959: 117).

The association with Georges Gaspard is tantalising since he was one of the true villains identified during the investigation of the 1931 Rebellion. Gaspard served as *Agent Territorial* from January 1926 until his death in November 1930 (Vanderstraeten 2001: 147, 14). He and his superior officer, Dewilliamort, regularly sent gangs of thugs to "recruit" men for the colonial army (*Force publique*) and (against official policy) for HCB. This collaboration went so deep that during a four-year period, the HCB recruiter never set foot outside his post since Gaspard and his superior provided all the men required (ibid.: 14). Equally despicable, Gaspard and Dewilliamort allowed HCB recruiters to seize livestock (chickens, goats and pigs) and pay the "government price", which was far below market value (ibid.: 14). Gaspard feathered his own nest by requisitioning huge quantities of livestock and agricultural products and selling them for his own profit at Kikwit (Sikitele 1986: 755-59). The quantities involved were such that Gaspard and Dewilliamort affected the health and nutrition of the entire region. If this were not enough, Gaspard routinely intervened in local politics. One of his actions directly linked to fomenting the rebellion was his imposition of an unpopular Chief Yongo, who capitalised on his association with the administration to exploit and brutalise his people (Vanderstraeten 2001: 14-15). The Pende nicknamed Gaspard "Attashio!" (Sikitele 1986: 755) in mocking remembrance of what must have been his constant angry refrain in French: "*Attention!*" ("Beware!")

Whether or not the European racing across the back of the chair actually portrays the notorious Gaspard, his activities make clear why a comparison to thieving leopards should resonate with viewers. Typically, Pende artistic strategies make use of composites to widen the semantic field. In this case, Muledi may have deliberately blurred the reading of bicycle and motorcycle in order to maximise the viewer's intuition of menace.

DIVINERS AS PATRONS

Among the Kwilu and Central Pende, diviners also emerged as important patrons for the arts (Strother 2000). Pende diviners are emphatically not "fortune-tellers". Instead, they seek to understand the historical roots for physical illness or social problems plaguing clients in the present. The most trustworthy of diviners are mediums chosen by the dead to serve as their mouthpiece during periods when the family suffers an unusually high rate of illness, death or other difficulties. Typically, mediums are women past menopause and they experience a short but intense career of maybe a year or two. They do not require payment and usually speak directly, without subterfuge, or elaborate ceremonies. Unfortunately, this precious gift is easily lost through ritual contamination or unethical behaviour. Consequently, most families in need have recourse to specialists (*nganga-ngombo*) who have learned their craft as part of their study of *wanga*, the manipulation of physical or metaphysical forces for personal advantage. The good faith of this second class of diviners (predominantly male) is deeply distrusted. Their performances can be highly theatrical. Often they speak in riddles and require multiple consultations. Their heavy fees have bankrupted more than one family. Because their clients are deeply sceptical, practitioners engage in a fierce competition for credibility. During the twentieth century, such diviners often sought to substitute what they lacked in a mandate from the dead by commissioning glamorous, mysterious objects, which promised powers rooted in long study and secret knowledge.

Two of the most renowned of such diviners' tools are the *galukoji* and *njinda*. The first *galukoji* known was collected in 1928 along the northern frontier and the practice probably spanned a generation of practitioners from the 1920s to the 1950s. The instrument is made of a series of intersecting bars of palm bamboo, about 30 cm long, which expand like accordions [fig. 8]. A small face is perched on the top of the first bar, facing outward. Usually, a coiffure of feathers or animal hair adorns the little head.

De Sousberghe described the *galukoji* as "frequently employed" among the Central Pende during his first field visit, 1951-53: "The diviner consulted usually lays the instrument on his knees, head up; he need only insert a finger somewhere in the crossbars so that at the desired moment, when the name of an individual suspected of evil spells is pronounced, the head will be projected upward, approaching his own: the oracle has thus designated the guilty party" (1959: 81; my trans.). The son of a practitioner at Nyoka-Kakese modified de Sousberghe's account. He described how his father would make assertions (You came because of such-and-so illness… Your grandmother respected certain *mahamba*…). If the client's representative accepted, the *galukoji* would jump out. This field associate emphatically denied that the *galukoji* would jump out to accuse someone for fear of inciting the individual's murder on the spot. The dramatic spring-like movement

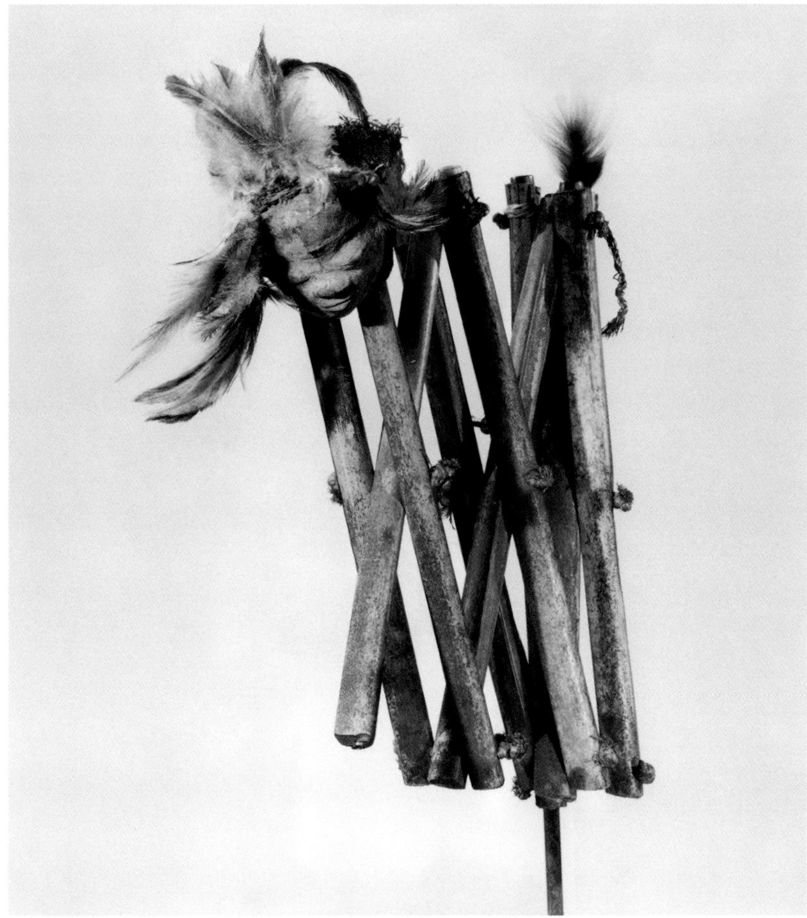

Fig. 8. Galukoji extended. H. 39.5 cm. Metropolitan Museum of Art,
no. 1976.410.1. Gift of Ruth Trunzo

of the *galukoji* in such an emotionally charged atmosphere would be too
explosive. This man's father last performed in 1948, and there was general
consensus that divination using the *galukoji* disappeared in the 1950s.

By far the most outstanding sculpture associated with a *galukoji* was
given to de Sousberghe as a present in 1953 by a diviner's widow. It depicts
a hyper-male physiognomy, narrow and peanut-shaped, with protruding
forehead, angled cheekbones, and pointy chin. The eyelids are pulled far to
the side towards the mandibular angle. There is a reference here to the
dangerous knowledge of the diviner; however, the bulging forehead also
accentuates the propulsive force of the outstretched, spring-like apparatus.

Another famous Pende divinatory tool is the *njinda*, which is directly
tied to the messianic uprising against the Belgians in 1931. The historian

Sikitele speculates that the Njinda or Nginda movement was of Lele origin, introduced through the mediation of neighbouring Wongo (1986: 957). In the 1920s, specialists developed divinatory tools in the unusual forms of power figures. Some report that the specialists circulated the charged statuette through the village, finally positioning it before the house of an accused sorcerer. If the work indicated guilt, the accused had the option of drinking a poison to affirm his innocence. The innocent were presumed to survive the ordeal by vomiting the poison (ibid.: 958). Some say that such statues were placed outside the village, neutralising antisocial practices within the community (ibid.: 959-60).

PI. 41

During the 1931 Rebellion, rumours circulated that one of the leaders, Matemu a Kelenge, used the *njinda* to consult the dead and promised protection for Pende soldiers through its power (de Sousberghe 1959: 150-51). Sikitele interviewed Father Jacqus Delaere, who collected an example in 1932-34 at Kamingilo, near the mission of Muhaku. He described the statuette as a type of "marionette" activated by the cords tied through its arms. The caretakers posed questions that could be answered by yes or no: if it fell in one direction, that was taken to mean "yes"; if it fell in the reverse direction, that meant "no". If it leaned forward, that meant something else entirely (1986: 961-62).

Five surviving *njinda* are known (Strother 2000b: 110-11). Imposing in stature, they stand between 100 and 116 cm high and bear numerous attachments in the forms of animal skins, beads, and tortoise shells. Although Kongo and Songye are renowned for power objects from the early twentieth-century composed according to an aesthetic of "accumulation" (Rubin 1974), this form is unprecedented in the Pende corpus. The figures conflate protruding, white-flashing male eyes with female breasts. There is always an antelope horn which shoots out of the top of the head and is presumed to be packed with medicinally charged earth. The arms of the statue are joined to the figure at the hips, creating a narrow opening through which strong ropes are tied around the arms. The figure confronts the viewer directly, standing on short, stout legs and wearing a short skirt.

The direct gaze of the figure and its white, protruding eyes underscore the aesthetic of fear informing the work. Twisted bushbuck horns are associated with practice of *wanga*. In this case, the upturned horn would be presumed (whatever the reality) to be packed with earth enriched with medicines made from various plants and animal parts as well as the grave-dirt or other materials used to "fix" a human spirit to activate the figure. Tortoise shells also are favourite medicine containers. Numerous strips of cloth were tied around the neck and waist of the figure. "Tying" is another prominent image in the manipulation of *wanga* and, in this context, implies the tight control by the caretakers of the forces channelled within the figure.

In the imagery associated with chiefly ritual houses, female forms predominate because women are presumed to have a greater capacity for loyalty and obedience than most men. In this representation, the youthful breasts convey both the protective capacities of the diviner's medicine and the firm control of this power by the diviner. A common tautological lesson of folklore is that the specialist who brings together certain physical and metaphysical powers eventually loses control of them so that he himself is consumed or injured. The female imagery assures the uneasy client that the human manipulation of forces cited in the horn and tortoise shell are under control and intended for good purposes.

As Wyatt MacGaffey explained for power objects in Kongo, these works were intended to provoke "astonishment" (1988). Among the Pende, they rarely survived a generation of practitioners as novelty was important to their ability to impress clients.

THE DECORATIVE ARTS

The visual arts are not exclusively religious among the Pende, nor have they been in the past. However, various historical developments have favoured the preservation, identification, and publication of ritual sculpture to the point where it is difficult to recover the full range of precolonial artistic expression. Works from early collections are more likely to be identified as "Pende" if they demonstrate motifs recognisably linked to known Pende masquerading traditions. Moreover, collectors were predisposed to value anthropomorphic works in the Pende corpus, and these all fell into the domain of the arts of the chief, related to his priestly function. Finally, the demands of forced labour during the colonial period had a swift and negative impact on the decorative arts in particular. For example, although Torday records a statement that the Bushongo (Kuba) learned embroidery from the Pende (1922: 347), very few textiles of assured provenance exist to substantiate this claim (Van Braeckel 1994). Most Pende ceased the time-consuming forms of cut-pile weaving shortly after contact. Consequently, we must look to basket-weaving to find some traces of this lost mastery in textiles. In 2006, most Eastern Pende import plain raffia cloth from the Wongo for ceremonial occasions. Furthermore, history has come full circle, because they rely on the Kuba to produce plush, "velvet" cloth, which they cut in fashionable designs for the hats, shirts and wrappers of chiefs.

Among the Kwilu Pende (and to a lesser extent, the Central Pende), men prized whistles as works of art. Usually carved in hard wood, they were made in an astonishing variety of forms (de Sousberghe 1959: fig. 132). By far, the most common use for whistles was in hunting, to call and direct dogs. Tukweso Donatien told de Sousberghe that in communal hunts, the men would use excited blasts from whistles both to terrify the game animals and push the dogs forward. However, certain Kwilu chiefdoms such as Mungindu, Mushinga, and Shimuna also kept certain whistles earmarked for war, many sculpted in ivory (letters to de Sousberghe dated 17 September and 26 October 1958). Depending on the quality of sound, other whistles were reserved for dances. For example, *shibidi* alternated pitch at an interval of a third and were associated with joyful events, such as village masquerades (Maquet 1954b: 9). Combined with ivory horns, iron bells and drums, they helped to create a distinctive texture of sound to accompany important chiefly rituals, such as the investiture of the chief or the construction of his house. The Kwilu Pende also used whistles to synchronise the dancing of the *Minganji* masks [fig. 2] and add to their intimidating presence.

Most Pende whistles had two openings, allowing for the creation of two tones, as the lateral orifice was opened or closed by a finger. In addition, the player could vary pitch, duration and interval. Since the Kipende language has two tones, the musicologist Maquet discovered that the player could manipulate the openings to mimic certain words, using the same logic as "talking drums". For example, hunters could communicate among themselves, mimicking words for "come here", "hurry", and "I'm coming". Town criers used whistles at night to alert the population to gather for important events the following day, for example, communal hunts. These whistles would alternate 1/8 notes followed by a higher 1/4 note. At dances, whistles could call masks onto the floor and praise exceptional performances by imitating the cry for "Bravo!" by giving two sounds at an interval of a third, with the second note higher (*Olo!*) (Maquet 1954b: 9). Whistles also exist with three openings, allowing for three to four tones, which were used in dance contexts. Maquet discovered that Kwilu Pende used whistles to replace the human voice in compositions with xylophones. He advised that whistles repay close examination to see the fine details of their manufacture, such as the double bevelling of a mouthpiece or the shaping of the orifice to be stopped to a particular finger (ibid.).

Apart from their role as musical instruments, Kwilu Pende fully aestheticised whistles as decorative pendants, and delighted in personalised, often playful compositions. Certain ivory whistles are modelled on old-fashioned barrel keys, which have a bit projecting from a hollow cylindrical shaft. The hollow shaft provides the main opening and a lateral orifice is carefully drilled through the bit on the side to provide the second note.

Pl. 44

Pl. 44

Two holes skilfully bored into the top of the coiffure allow for the object to be strung as a pendant. The transformation of a key into a whistle is not as curious as it might first appear. Frans Olbrechts observed that Belgians amused themselves by holding keys to their lips and whistling across the hollow barrel (de Sousberghe 1959: 84). The Pende artist has punned on the large "bow" (or round handle for the key) to create a head with long braids drawn from the fashionable *mukoto* hairdress (also illustrated in Petridis 2002: fig. 3).

Pl. 32

Collectors know that pendants appeal to the hand as well as to the eye. They fit nicely into the palm and Pende appreciate how ivory feels cool to the touch, no matter how hot the day. Part of its attraction derives from the way that the thumb glides over its lustrous surface. In fact, professional sculptors treat ivory with special preparations, seeking to inhibit cracking and increase its shine. The smoother the surface, the better (and cooler) it feels. This particular whistle is exceptionally lightweight and offers the hand contrasts of texture and glossy smoothness.

Pende also cherish ivory as a medium for its whiteness and, in jewellery, for the contrast it makes against brown skin [fig. 9]. Owners of such works string the pendants around their necks, where in the course of the day they pick up sweat and (in the past) a red tint from the bark powder used as skin conditioner. If placed in storage, they also can become discoloured from house smoke. Although Westerners prize a golden patina, many Pende waged an endless war against time as they fought to preserve the ivory's original whiteness as long as possible. They did so by scrubbing the objects regularly (even daily) with fine, abrasive sand whenever they went to bathe at the local stream.

Because of the patina on some of these key-whistles, de Sousberghe attributes their origin to contact with the Portuguese before the establishment of the colonial state (1959: 84). However, in my experience, a beautiful patina can date from only a decade of use (especially when the object is cleaned regularly with sand). There seems to be no reason to suppose that any of these works date before the establishment of the Congo Free State, especially since they depict hairstyles fashionable in the early colonial period and none have ever been described in Angola. The colonial state banned hunting in the Kwilu and other social changes undermined the market for decorative whistles. Carving the whistles required sophisticated skills to achieve the desired qualities of sound in addition to the finesse of working ivory on a miniaturised scale. When Tukweso Donatien tried to find sculptors with the requisite skills in order to commission whistles for de Sousberghe in 1958, he discovered that most had died before or during the 1931 Rebellion. Although some Central Pende sculptors continued to work after the Rebellion, 1931 forms the *terminus ante quem* for the most accomplished works.

If whistle-pendants began to disappear in the 1930s, other ivory pendants depicting widespread Central Pende masks enjoyed an extraordinary popularity lasting until Independence in 1960. Emil Torday already noted their widespread use during his visits along the northern frontier of the Kwilu and Central Pende, 1906-09. He wrote that the miniature masks (*mbuya*) "are made of wood or ivory and are considered to be talismans by their owners; they may be worn only by adult men, although inferior copies in ivory, wood, or metal may be worn by anyone, even women" (1922: 331; my trans.). De Sousberghe describes the pendants as "amulets" and states that some men wear examples in ivory whereas other men, as well as women and children, wear cruder copies made from wood or seeds (ibid.: 73-74). Both Torday and de Sousberghe document pendants made from a wide range of metals (copper, zinc, brass, tin, lead, and aluminium) (Torday and Joyce 1922: 351; de Sousberghe 1959: 75).

Pl. 45

Some of the contradictions in the literature over who may wear pendants and why is reinforced by a disposition to see all African art as religious in motivation (Rodolitz 2003). Recent fieldwork has clarified the issue. If a diviner diagnoses that a man or a child (often male) has fallen ill because the family has allowed a mask to lapse that an "uncle" once performed, the neglected ancestor will be pacified by the victim's wearing a miniature mask to show that the ancestor's achievements have not been forgotten. Eventually, the full-scale mask must be danced, but until the desired performer is old enough or strong enough, a miniature will suffice. The Eastern Pende know only this amuletic use of miniature masks, which they call *paku*. For example, when Chief Kingange's wife suffered from terrible nightmares as a child, the diviner revealed that her mother's father, who had been a famed dancer of Kambanda (the female mask), was angered that his legacy had been forgotten. The diviner made her a miniature of Kipoko (which represents all of the village masks), which she wore throughout her youth. Meanwhile, the family took the responsibility of sponsoring a dancer of Kambanda at regular intervals. In Eastern Pende practice, women also wore miniatures of Kipoko hidden around their hips when they suffered from miscarriages or other problems attributed to related causes.

Pl. 8

The material or skill used to carve the miniature masks prescribed by the diviner is not significant because they were intended to serve only as temporary substitutes for a proper masquerade figure. Most are carved by amateurs (by the father or diviner) from materials at hand, whether a stick of wood or even a seed or a nut. While it is possible that someone might commission an example in ivory from a sculptor, field associates stress that the vast majority of pendants in ivory or hippo bone were purchased for reasons of beauty (*ginango*). Although one must presume that the diviners' miniatures inspired the form of the decorative pendant, and the term for both is the same (*ikhokho*, lit. "carved things") among the Kwilu and Central Pende, dozens of field associates among the Kwilu Pende, North-central, and Central Pende were unanimous and even vehement that the pendants carved for beauty in ivory should not be confused with the crude affairs hacked out by amateurs during periods of illness. Instead, elephant ivory or hippo bone were confided to the most experienced of sculptors to make miniatures of village masks to enhance their clients' sense of beauty and style. Why masks? Because the Pende still regard them as their highest art form.

In the late 1980s, many (but not all) field associates initiated before 1931 claimed that women might also wear *ikhokho* carved from ivory. They explained that they did so less frequently simply because women did not have access to the same resources as men. Consequently, when they wore the ivories, they were often borrowed from male relatives. However, miniatures prescribed by diviners disappeared during the 1990s and this development seems to have influenced beliefs on who should wear *ikhokho*. Increasingly, field associates argue that the pendants depict masks, which are the purview of men, and therefore it would be inappropriate for women to wear their reproductions. The reasons for wearing *ikhokho* have also changed. Whereas the historical record (and my personal experience) demonstrates that many men wore pendants on a daily basis, increasingly they are reserved for festive occasions highlighting "traditional" dress [fig. 9]. In the words of one sculptor in 2006, "we wear [them] at times of joy, especially during dances, in order to embellish [the event]".

Pl. 45

Plate 45 represents the most common form of ivory pendant, which depicts a generic male face, merging the features of the older face masks slanting off the forehead (with unpierced eyes) with the coiffure adapted for Fumu or Pumbu. One sculptor reasoned that female masks are never represented simply because their hairstyles would not reproduce well. Less frequently, Giwoyo or Muyombo are depicted [fig. 9]. The miniatures are carved with extremely sharp features because the sculptors fully understand the abrasive effect of many years of sand baths. Plate 43 and 45 show the effect of several years' of care: the protruding eyelids, nose, and mouth have been softened. However, plate 46 demonstrates the logical extreme of years of fighting the wages of time—the features of the face and the hands appear to melt away before our eyes as the figure is subsumed to its essential core. Comparisons with works in the field indicate that this work received *fifteen to twenty years* of sand baths. The original owner has left a trace of his own long-abiding fascination for this carving in the transformation of its surface.

Pl. 15

Pl. 19, 21

Pl. 43, 45

Pl. 46

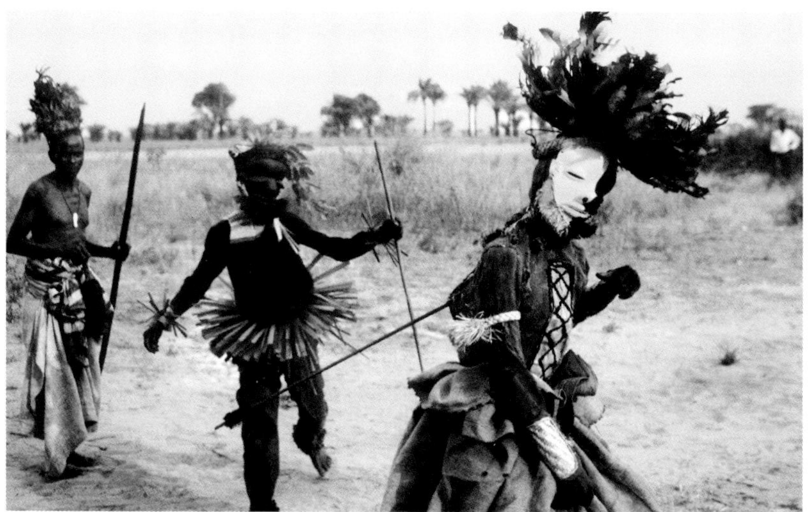

Fig. 9. Khoshi Mahumbu dances the mask Mbangu. Note the arrow piercing the masker's humpback. An audience member (left) wears an ivory pendant. Nyoka-Munene, DRC, 1989. Photograph: Z. S. Strother

Pende arts of personal adornment also included filed teeth, elaborate hairstyles for both men and women, and cicatrisations for women [fig. 7]. Hairstyles became a source of silent contention in the wake of the 1931 Rebellion. Belgian administrators and missionaries refused to hire men unless they cropped their hair, claiming that elaborate styles encouraged people to be lazy when they should be increasing production for the state. In response, more Pende than ever began to dress their hair. Foreigners fretted over the defiance (Strother 1998: 261). In 1953, Maquet observed the continuance of indigenous hairstyles and red-tinted skin lotions (unusual in the colony by this point). He wondered at the fact that many Pende were willing to adopt bicycles and phonographs, but not Western clothes (1953: 1). Ironically, traditional hairstyles and dress went definitively out of fashion at Independence, when the greater problem became how to lay claim to Congolese citizenship.

The selective "traditionalism" that the Central Pende constructed in the wake of the 1931 rebellion became a tool to needle the invaders even as it reminded the people of who they were. The extraordinary popularity of decorative ivory pendants from the 1930s–1950s should be situated within this historical framework as an act of political resistance. In addition to "beauty", the pendants asserted a "Pende" identity that was itself a product of modernity.

How Did Pende Works of Art End Up in Western Collections?
Igor Kopytoff has suggested that one might write the "biography of a thing"
by posing some of the same questions that one "asks about people", such
as: "What are the recognised 'ages' or periods in the thing's 'life'…? How
does the thing's use change with its age, and what happens to it when it
reaches the end of its usefulness?" (1986: 66-67). So far this essay has examined
why Pende commission works of art and how their differing audiences view
them. A variety of "biographies" have emerged for the objects depending
on how they are situated within a nexus of social relationships. For example,
the close identification of fraternity masks with initiates has direct consequences on when the masks are commissioned, who may wear them, and how
they interact with an audience of non-initiates. And yet, what happens when
the initiation ends? Kopytoff suggests important questions that are neglected
in the African art literature on the mortality and malleability of works of art.

Near the end of the initiation, Eastern Pende boys once burned fraternity masks in huge bonfires on a moonless night, enjoying the hiss and pop
of the dried wood. The destruction dramatically signalled the end of this
unique, liminal period in the boys' lives. More recently, the masks have been
reserved for sale to the foreign market. Sometimes the tips of their horns
are cut off. As a substitute, chiefs give the boys burlap sacks full of blocks of
wood to throw into the fire. What is important is that the masks disappear
never to be seen again. Each *mukanda* must be dedicated to a new generation,
fresh and individualised. Gifting used works soaked in other boys' sweat
would not be loving or respectful.

Dancers serve as the patrons for most of the village masks, with the
exception of Kipoko and Pumbu, which always belong to the chief. Most of
the headpieces have a relatively short lifespan because they are carved from
light wood to facilitate performance. They crack easily, at which point they will
be discarded. Masquerades honour the dead and it would hardly be rever-
ential to display blemished or discoloured sculptures. Because the headpiece
is only part of the masquerader's ensemble, it is not judged dangerous and
may be disposed by throwing it in the bush (often on a termite mound). In
this case, the act of destruction is not significant in and of itself. Selling the
work also constitutes an acceptable (and popular) form of disposal.

Not everyone willingly accepts ephemerality. There are documented
cases when a chief or dancer so admires the artistry of a mask (which he has
personally commissioned) that he carefully preserves the object away
from house smoke and termites. I have seen works over ten years' old that
look as though they were carved yesterday. The performer will freshen the

colours before each performance. The lustre of the patina visible in plate 25 derives from the build-up of many layers of paint and indicates that this face mask was danced repeatedly. On rare occasions, the patron refuses to accept that the "mask has died" (*mbuya yafua*) and will try to make a repair. One Kipoko mask illustrates such an intervention. The original owner carefully carved and painted a stopper to plug a hole in order to extend the work's life. Careful repairs such as this testify to the owner's deep affection for a singular artistic interpretation.

The sculptures surrounding the chief's house are implicated in a struggle for control between the chief and his people that directly affects the life history of these objects. The sculptures encrusting his house or hidden inside, figurated stools and chairs, staffs, and chiefly regalia, all are regarded with a certain fascination, a certain wariness sometimes verging on dread. The statuary offers comfort by advertising spirit sentinels watching over the community while arousing anxiety that the same works may shield the chief if he decides to pursue political power (like Kombo in the story). For this reason, architectural sculptures normally have a defined lifespan (rarely more than a decade) before they are put into harm's way, left to decay, or sold out of the community. At such time, the spirits captured are released and allowed to continue their journey to the otherworld. Figurated chiefly regalia are rarely inherited and may be allowed to decay in his house after his death. By these means, the community assures that such powerful objects may not be usurped for personal ends, at least not for long.

Twentieth-century diviners among the Central and Kwilu Pende sought to lure sceptical clients through the manipulation of glamorous or mysterious instruments. Because of intense competition, the forms for these works were continually reinvented and ranged from simple horns to large-scale power objects. Because each diviner promised a new and improved method, few of their instruments proved popular for more than a generation. At the end of the diviner's career, or on his death, such works might be left on his grave or allowed to deteriorate within his abandoned house. Increasingly, during the twentieth century, such works were sold or given to outsiders by heirs who did not choose to keep close at hand objects whose composition they did not understand.

The biographies described above for Pende sculptures are rooted in the particularities of the relationship of the patron to the work. However, by this point, it should become clear that these histories routinely include a moment of transformation when the work enters the international market, where it is redefined as an anonymous commodity, as a "work of art" valued for its formal qualities, its age, and its ability to embody cultural difference.

This is no new development. Pende sculptors responded *immediately*, on contact, to an expanded market for their works (Schildkrout 1998: 184; Fabian 1998). The earliest collections indicate that Pende art has been fully integrated into the world market throughout the twentieth century (Strother 1999).

From one perspective, this relationship might be regarded as a fruitful symbiosis. Since few works of art were inherited, masks and chief's sculptures may be released freely when they have outlived their designated lifespan. Since *mukanda* masks cannot be passed onto the next generation, selling them instead of burning them helps subsidise the heavy expenses incurred by the chief in hosting the initiation. Pende often joke about the peculiar preference of foreigners for used, even cracked and discoloured sculptures. In this case, they are able to enjoy the masks during the initiation period and then pass them along to a new audience, which values signs of use. Sometimes the impact of this foreign taste has changed practice. For example, fewer owners of pendants are cleaning them with sand to preserve their whiteness because they understand full well the commodity value of patina. Instead, they have come to regard the pendants as an investment to be husbanded against a rainy day.

On the other hand, we must acknowledge that all too often severe financial pressures force patrons to relinquish their works before they would have wished in order to pay debts. These include international developments as well as private misfortunes, including rubber quotas and taxes imposed by the colonial regime or hikes in school fees triggered by policies of the International Monetary Fund for the repayment of foreign loans. The commodification of sculptures also incites theft and has changed the cultural landscape. In 2006, I found that many Eastern Pende chiefs had begun to keep carved door panels and lintels inside their houses and only extract them on special occasions. As a consequence, fewer works of quality are on public display.

Since the late 1980s (if not earlier), many Pende sculptors have fantasised about seeing their sculptures displayed in museums associated with their names. Sadly, the artist's name has been stripped from most Pende objects as part of a strategy to assign precolonial value (Strother 1999: 30-31). However, cultural biography reveals that very few Pende sculptures date before 1900. Some of the most renowned are unquestionably mid-century. Consequently, such works are embedded directly in experiences of colonialism, Independence, and post-colonial struggles. Respecting the biography of these works is a means to reintroduce them into twentieth century history and to the lives and aspirations of their makers.

PLATES

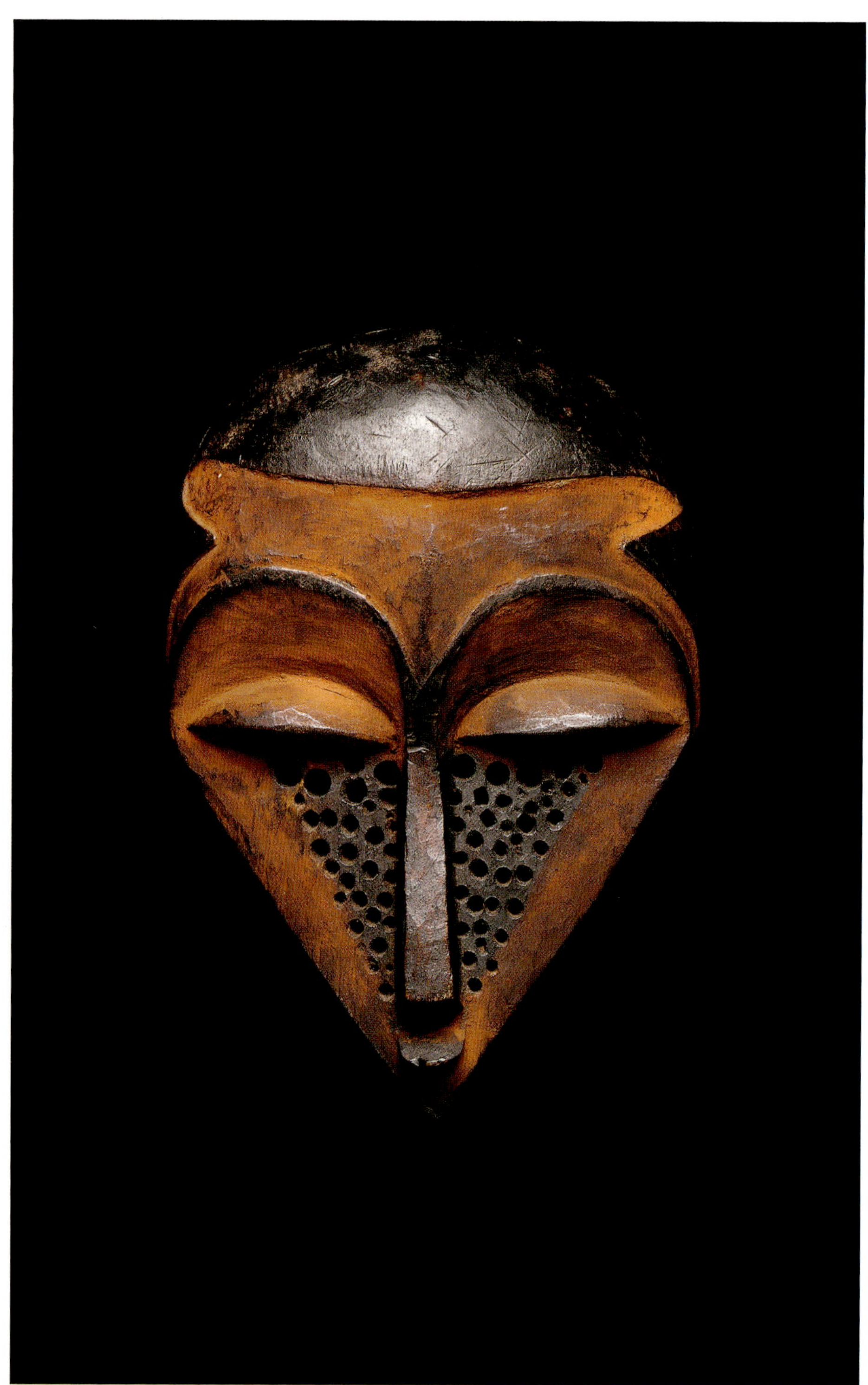

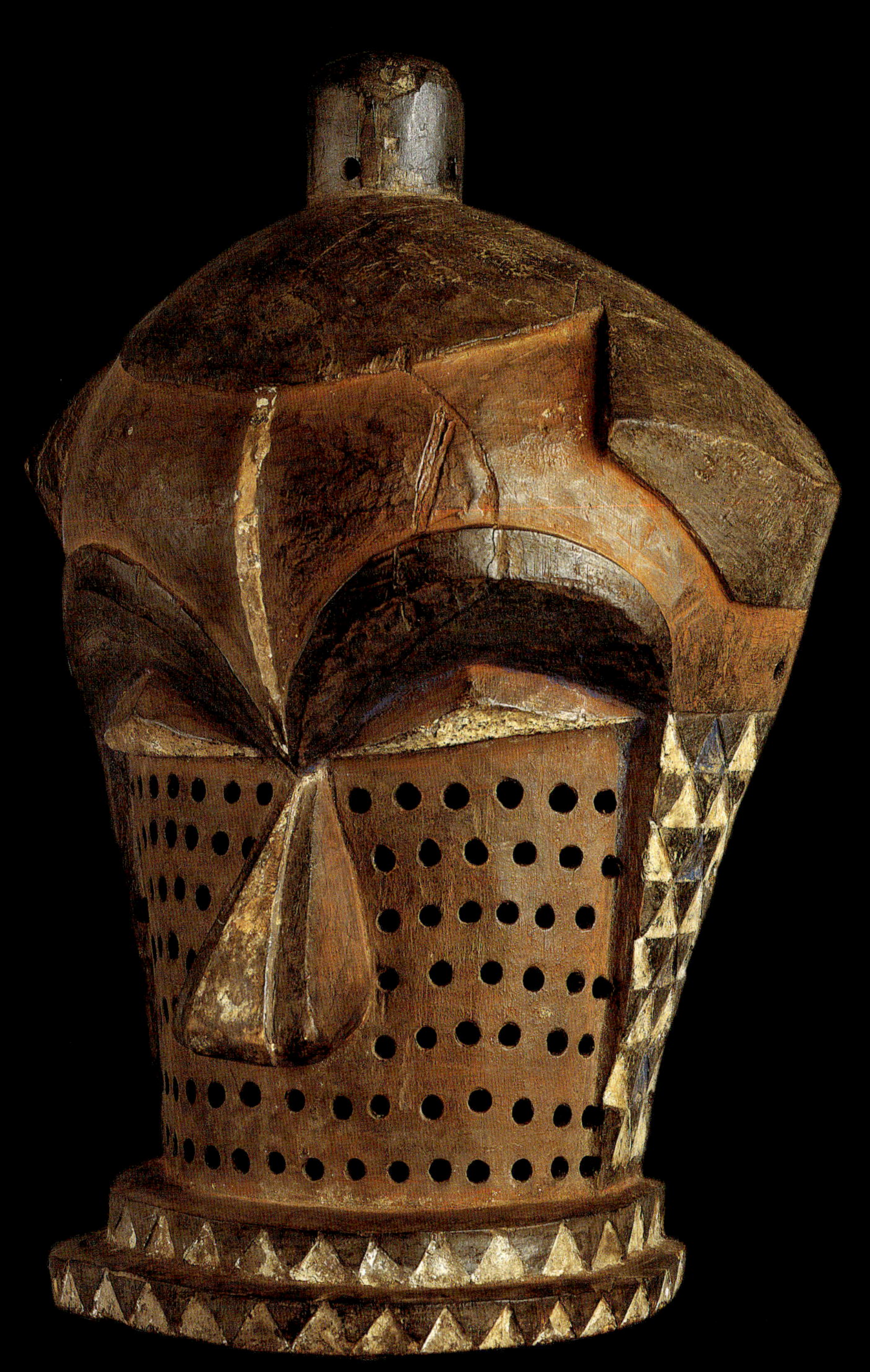

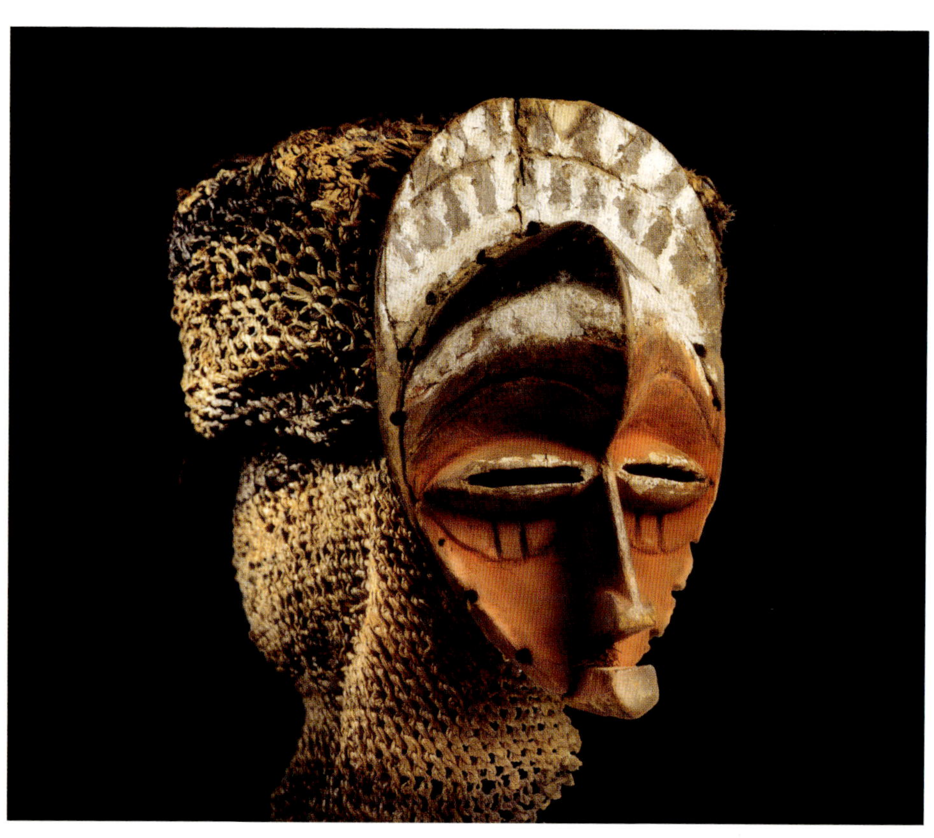

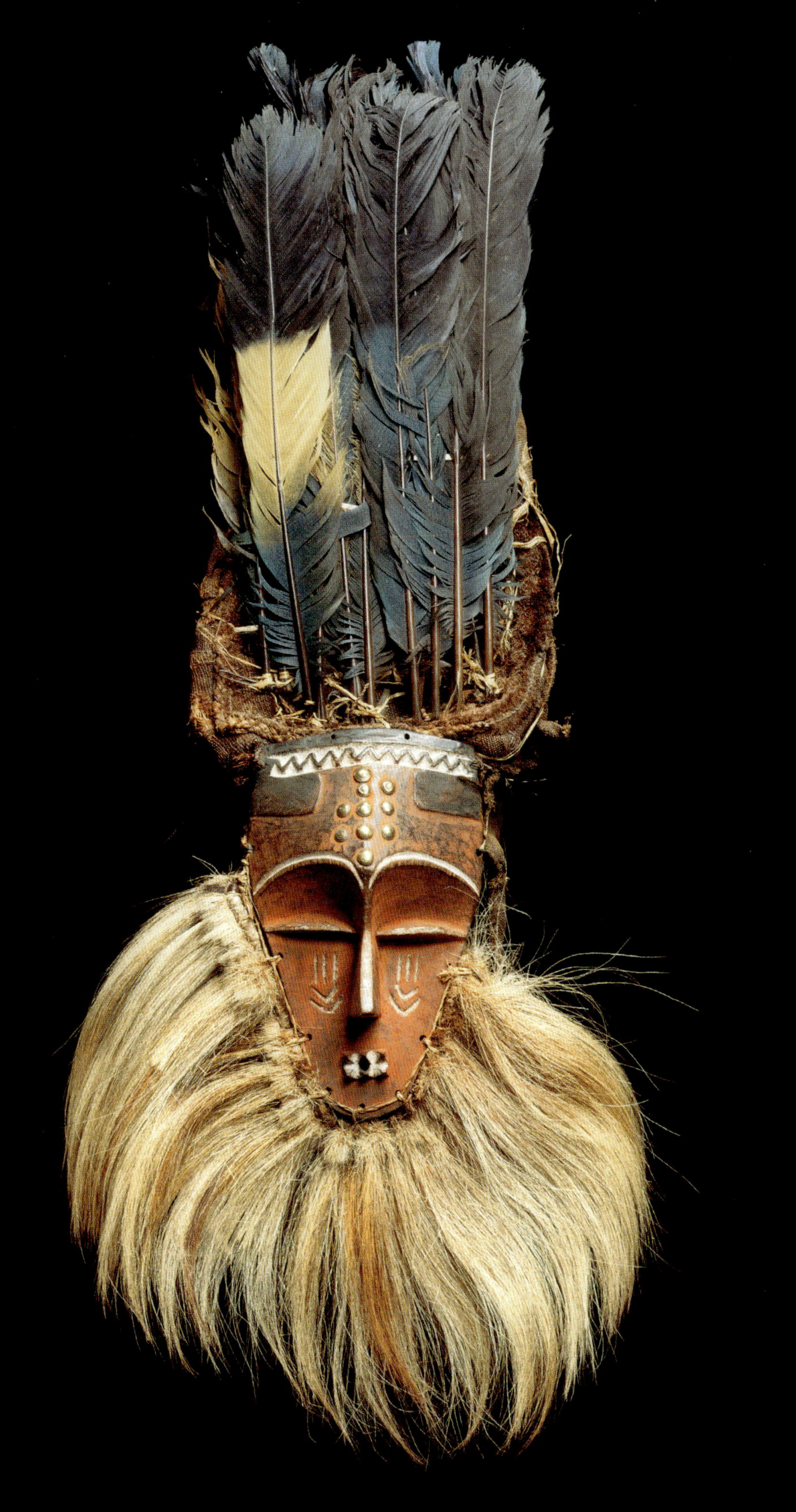

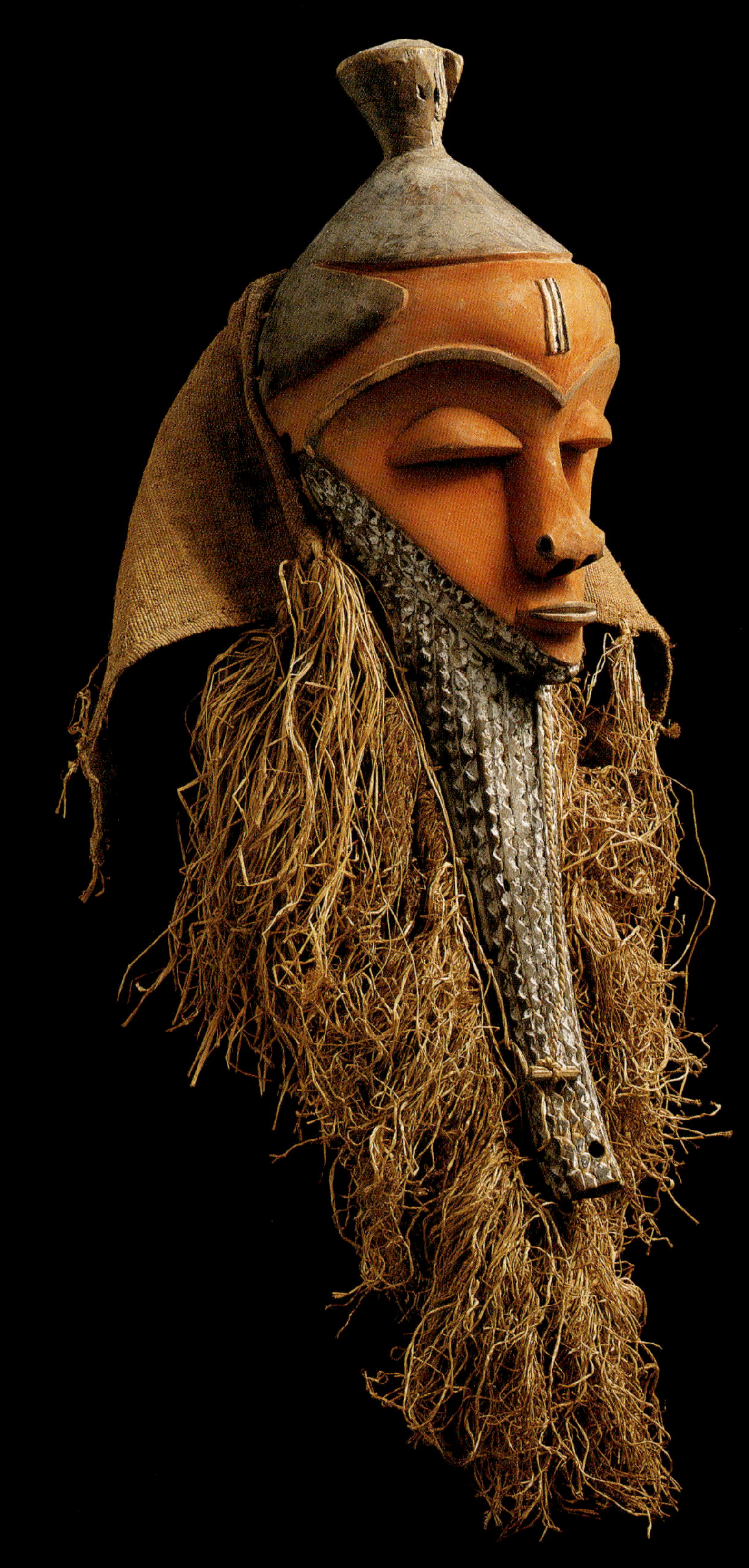

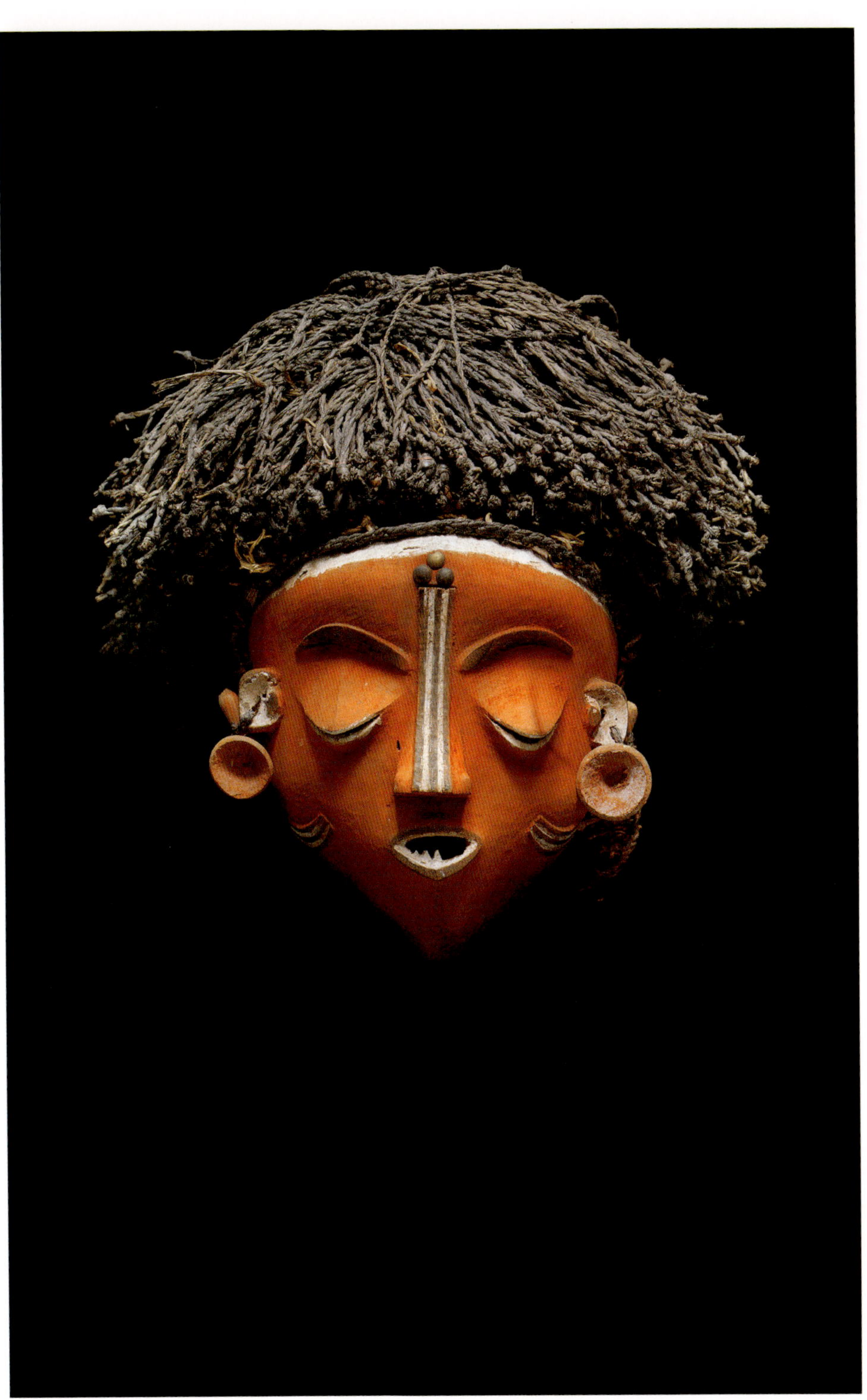

5 - 6 I 7 - 8

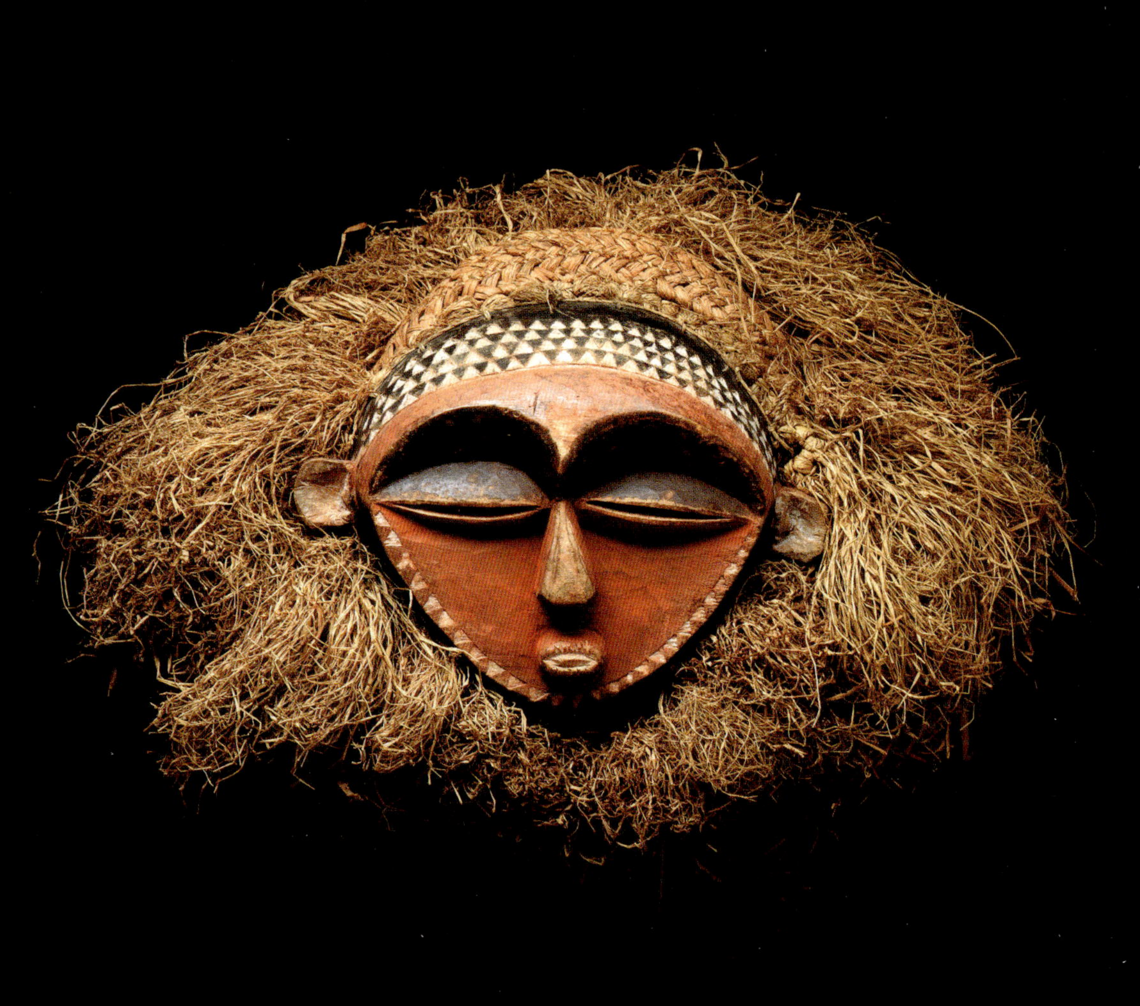

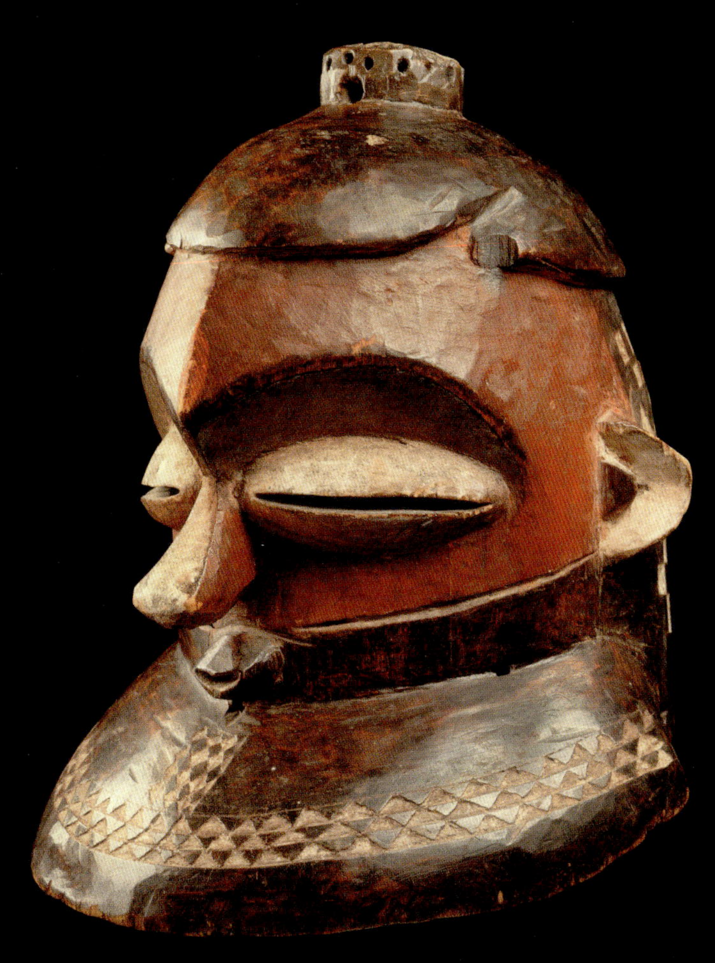

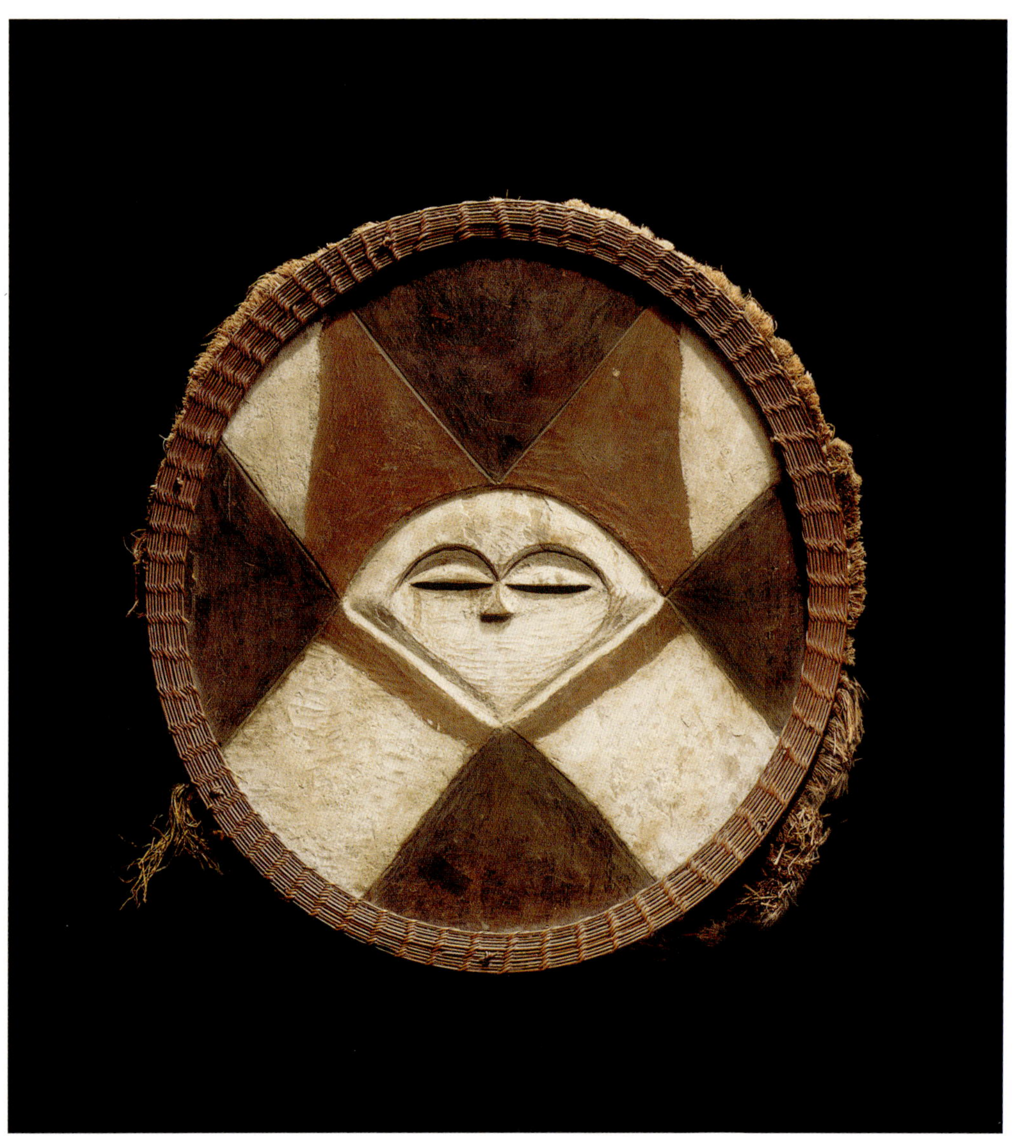

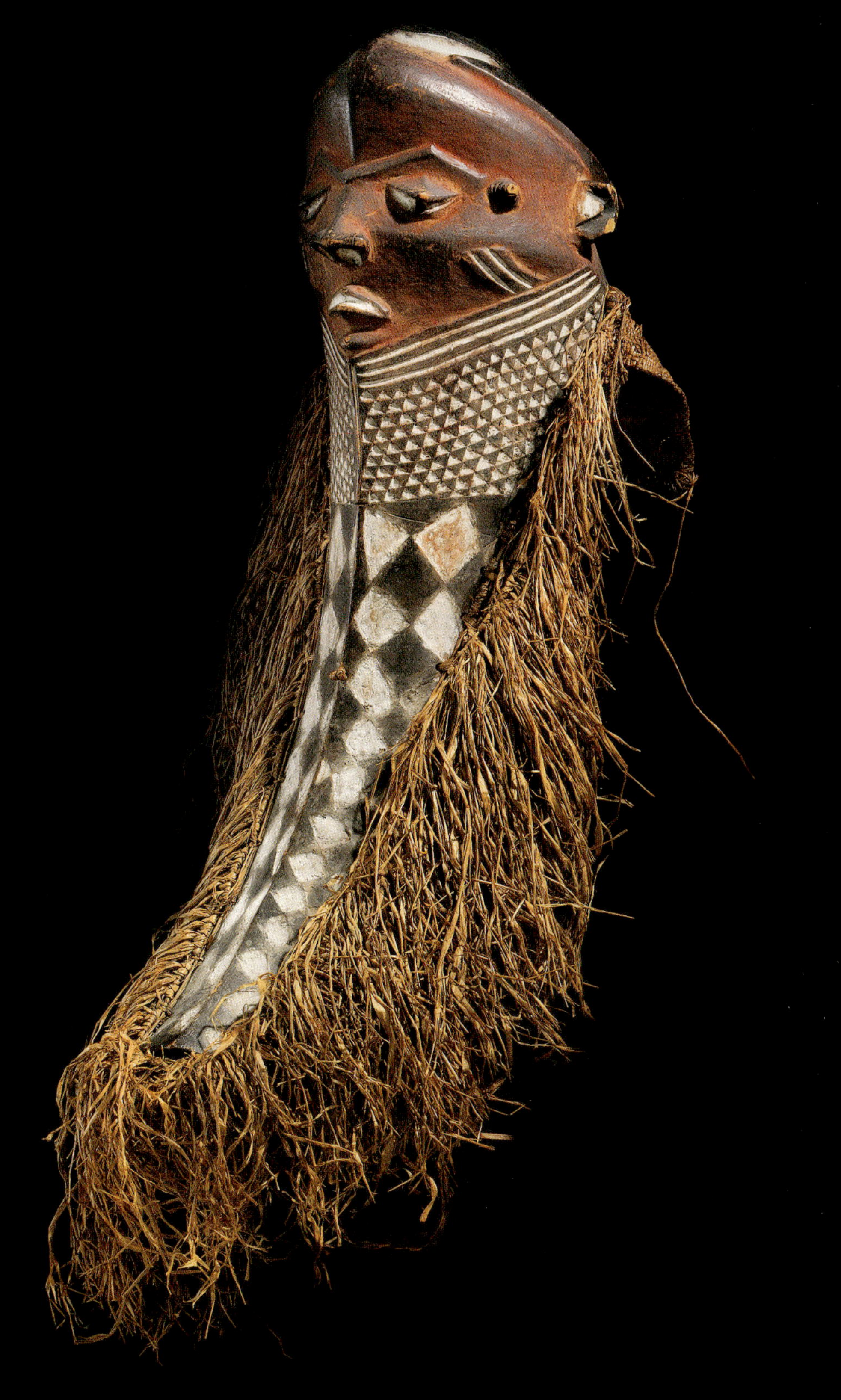

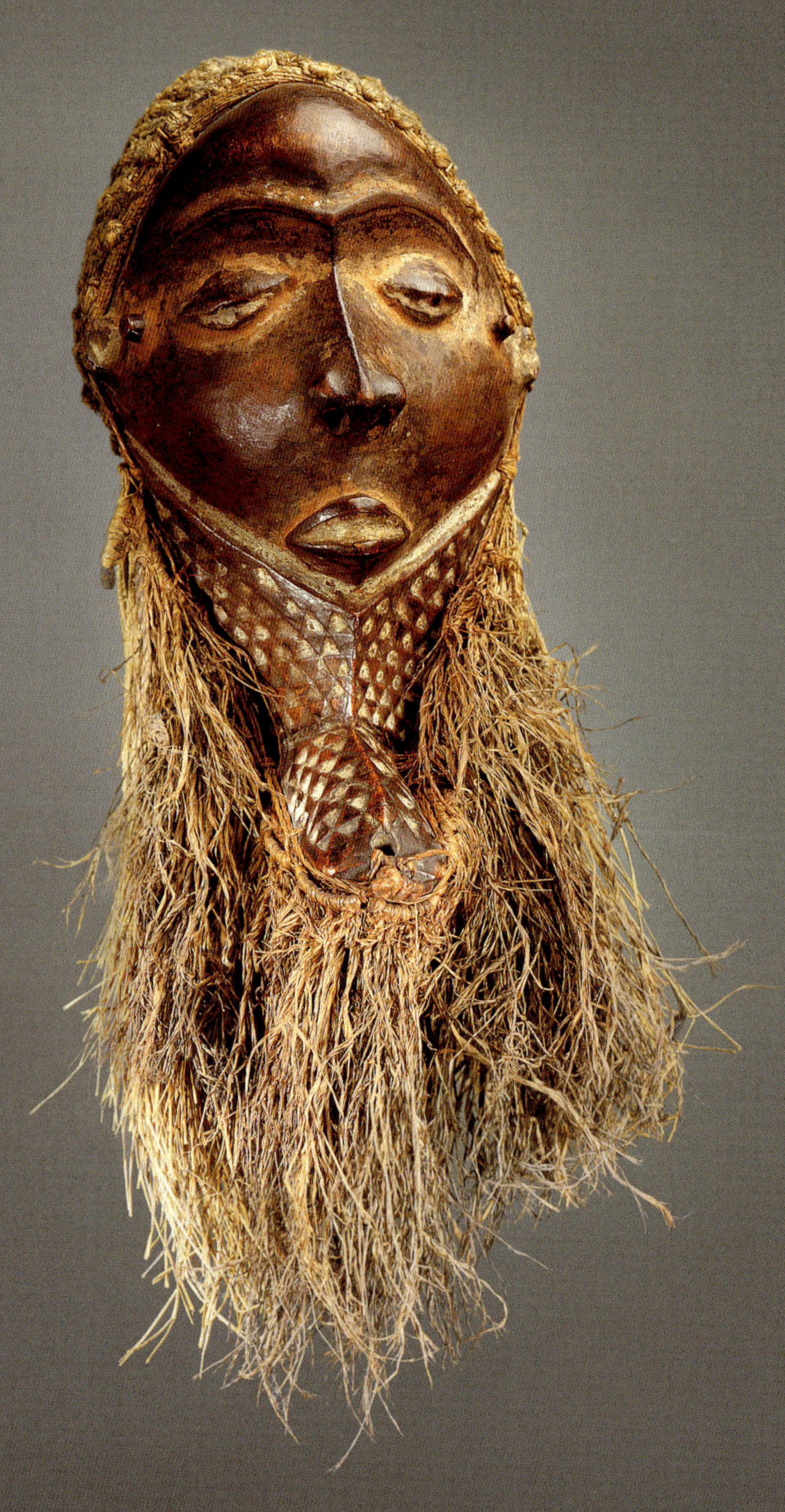

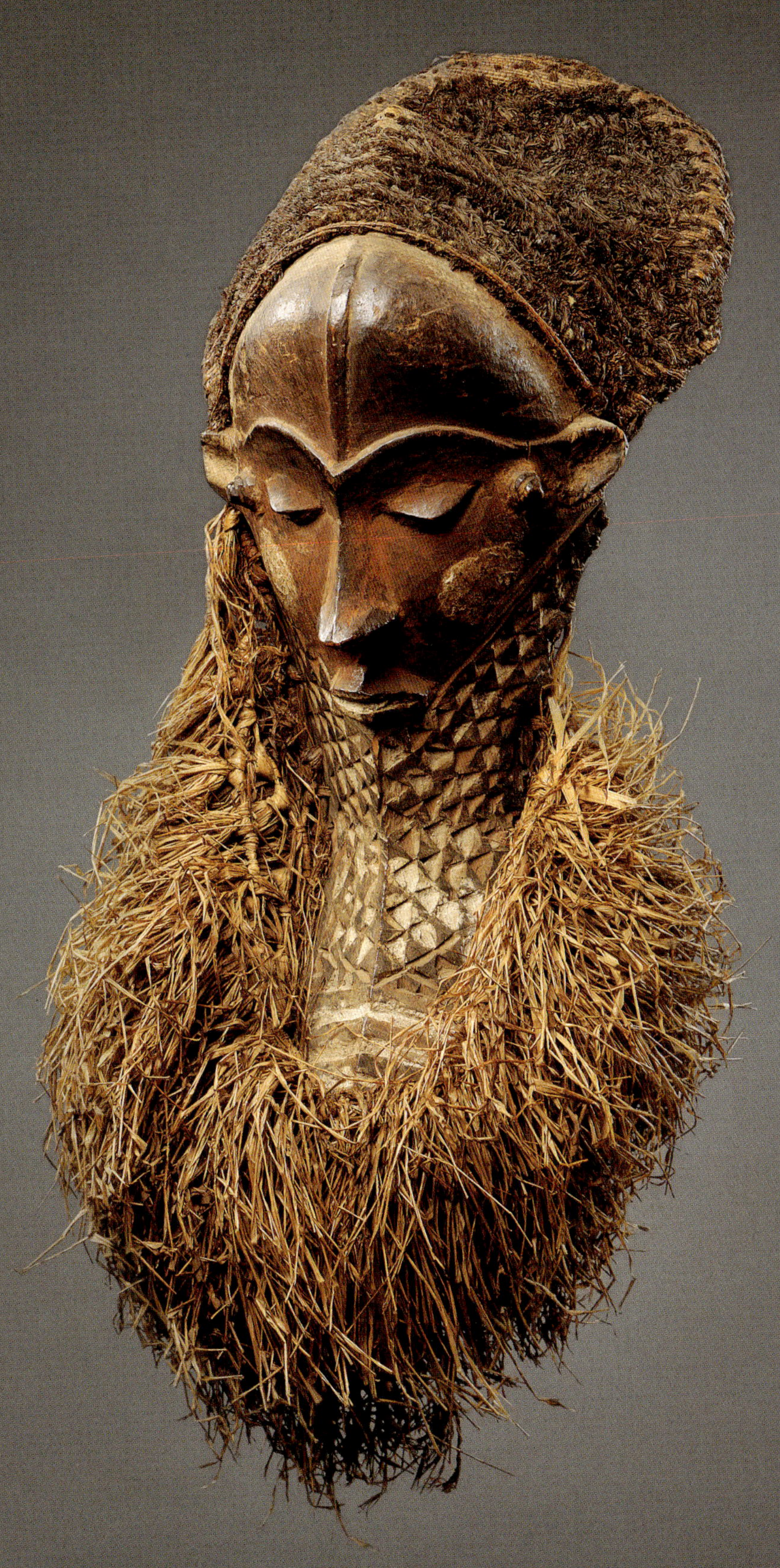

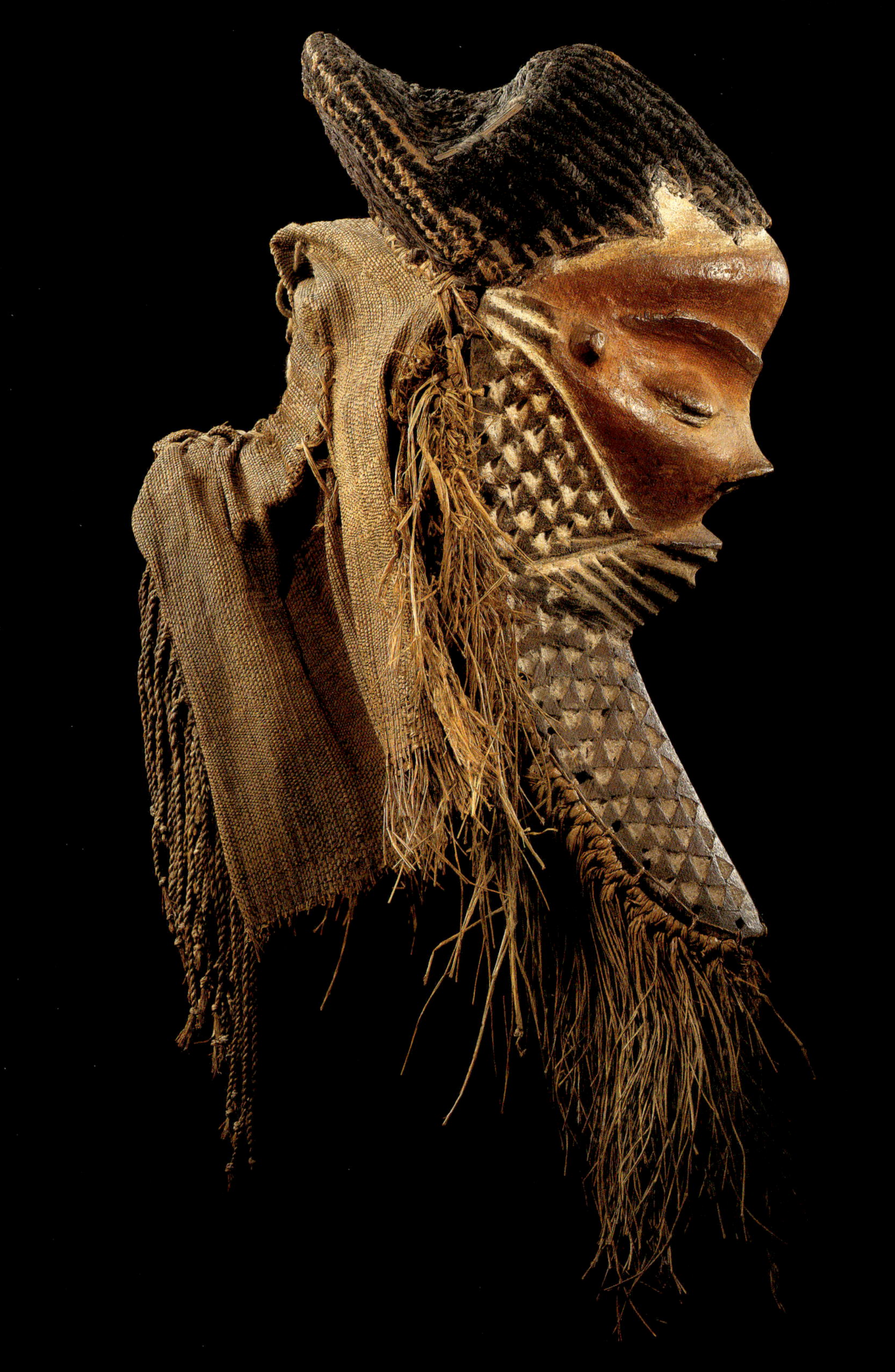

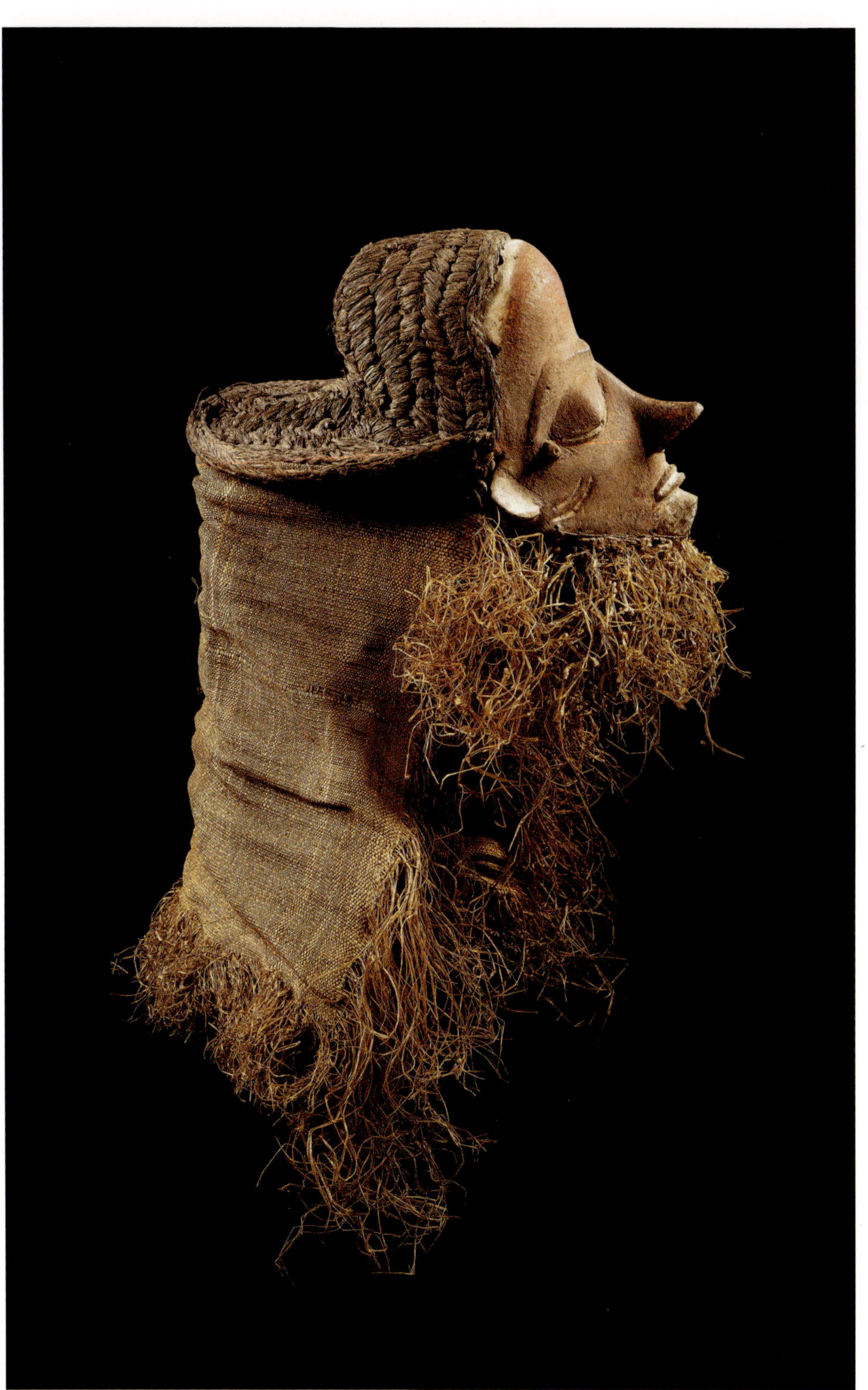

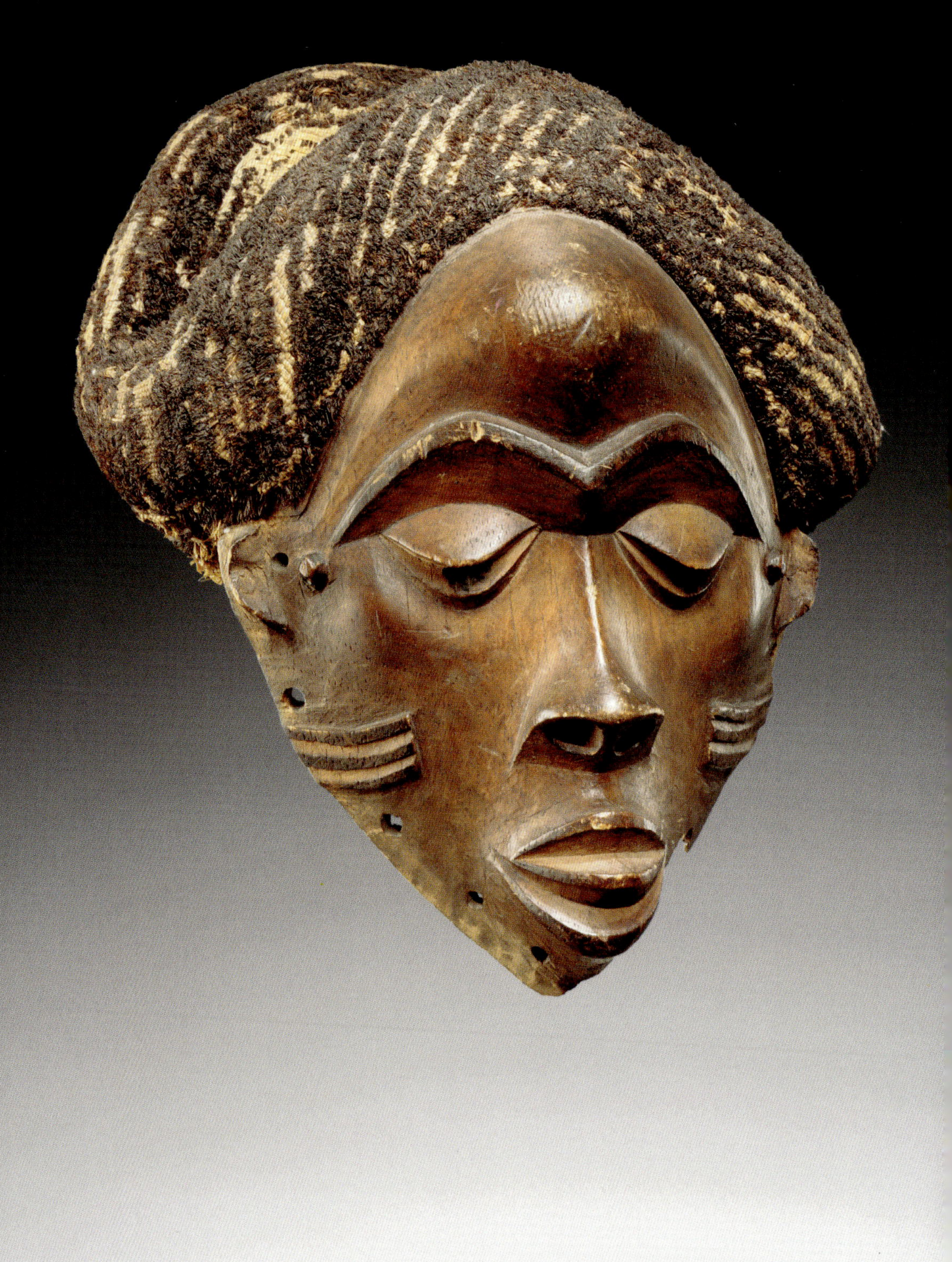

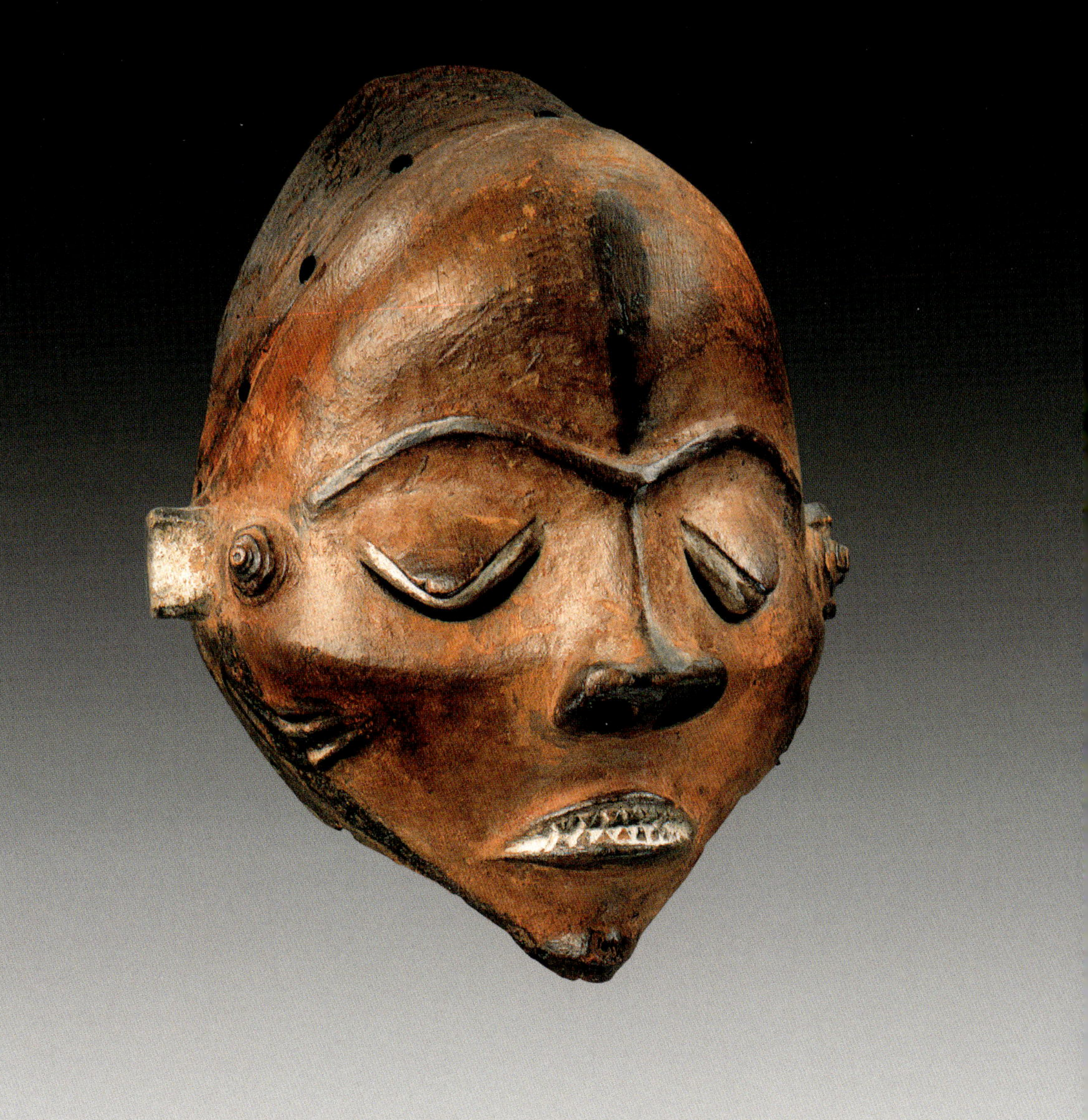

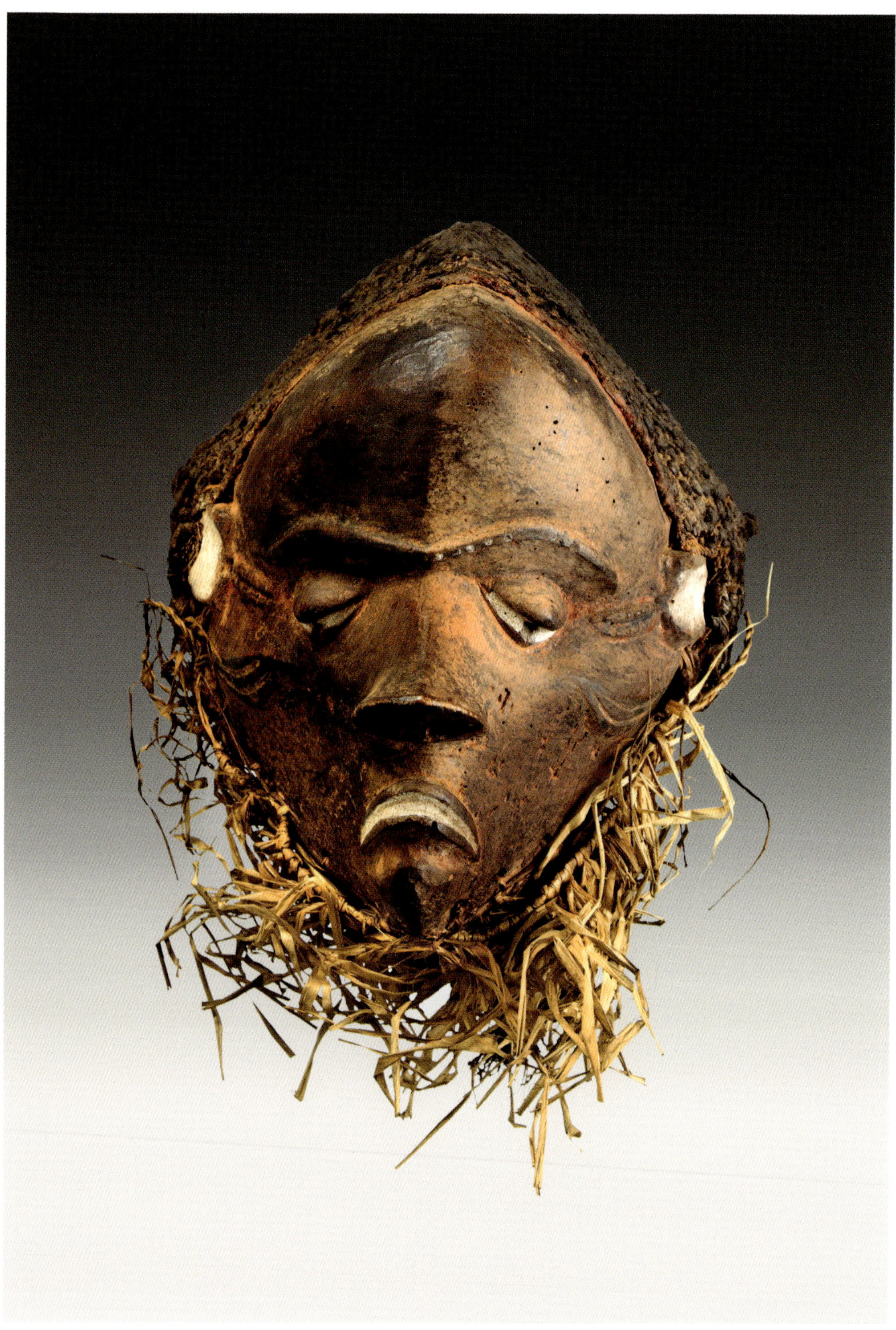

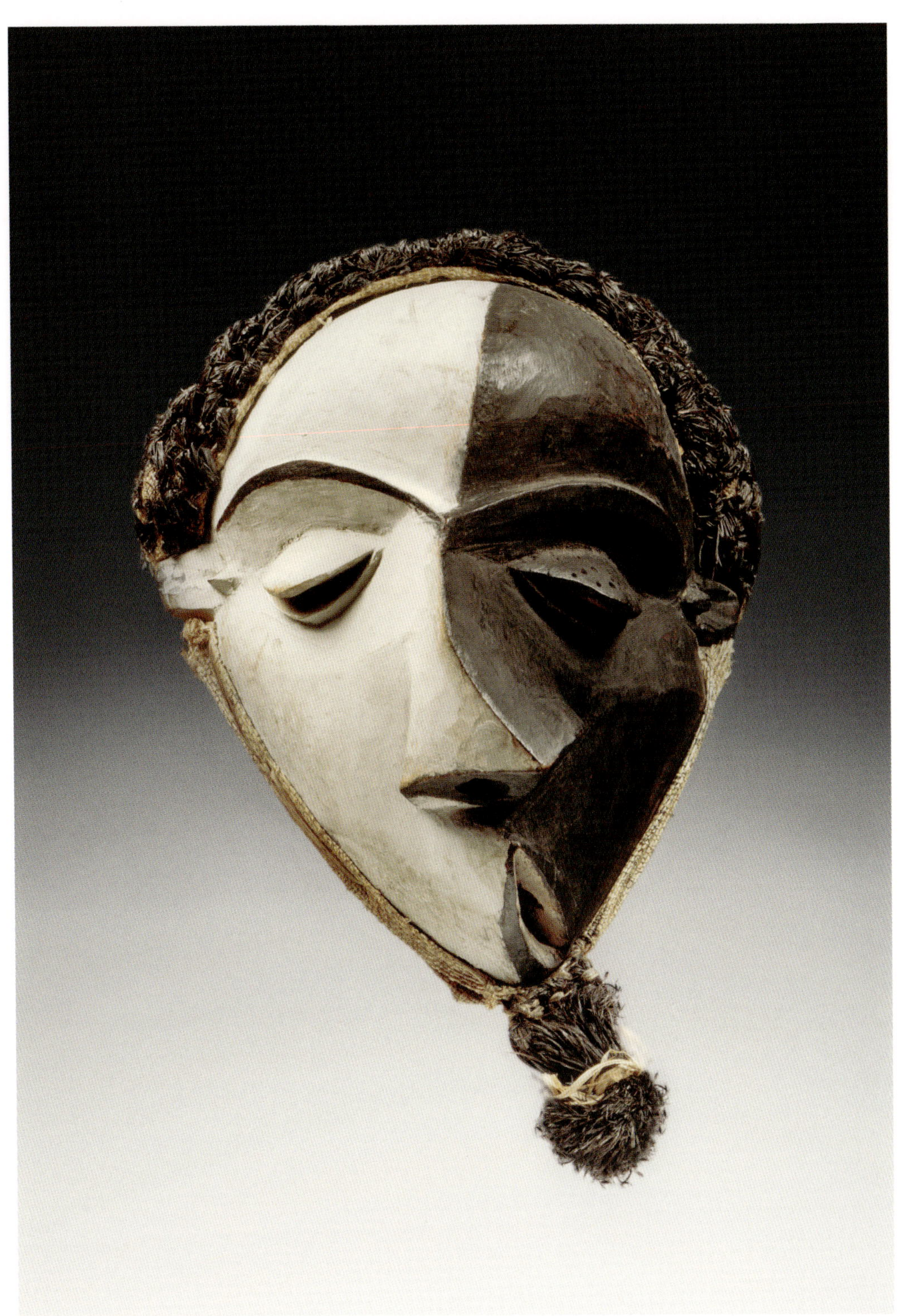

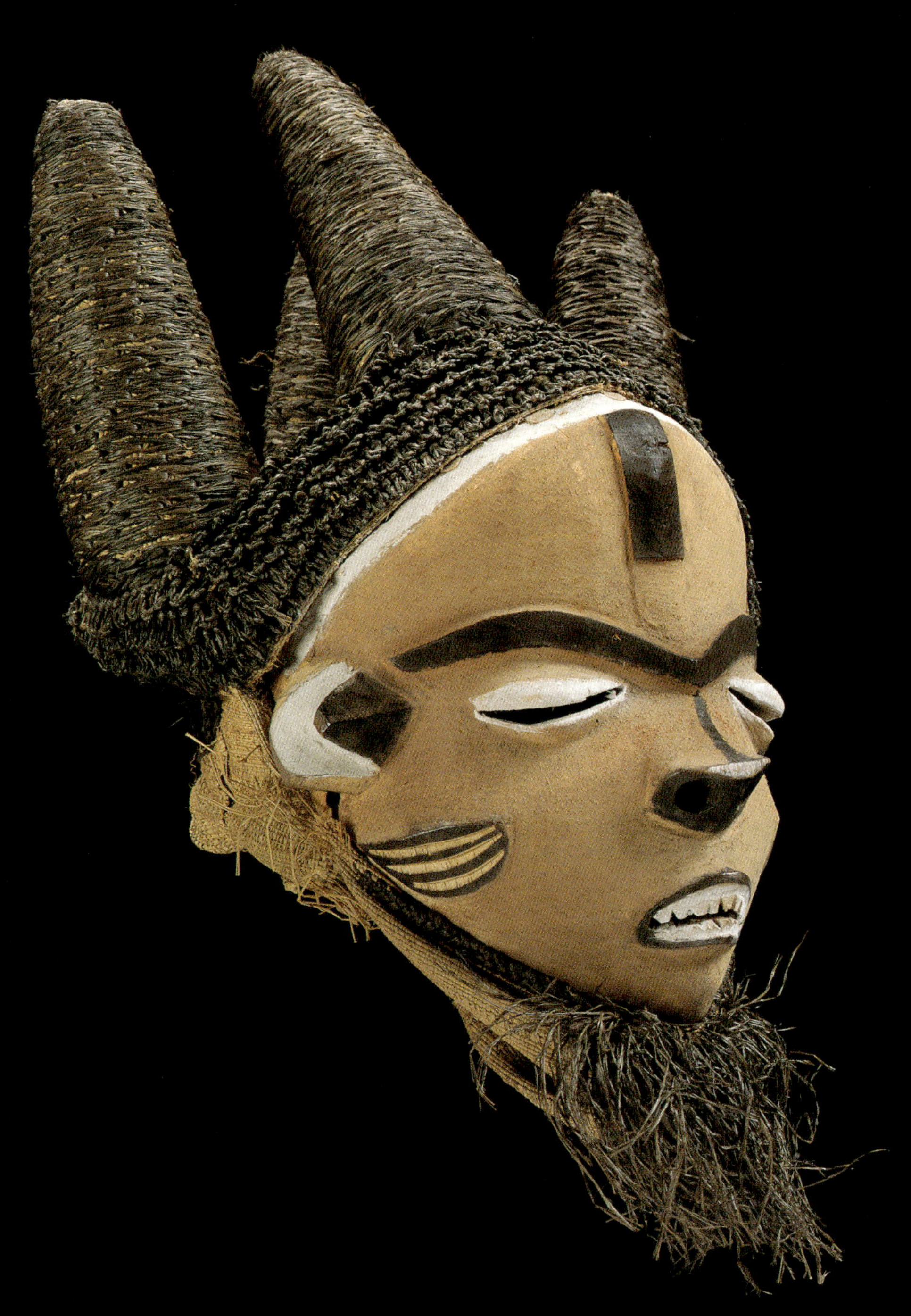

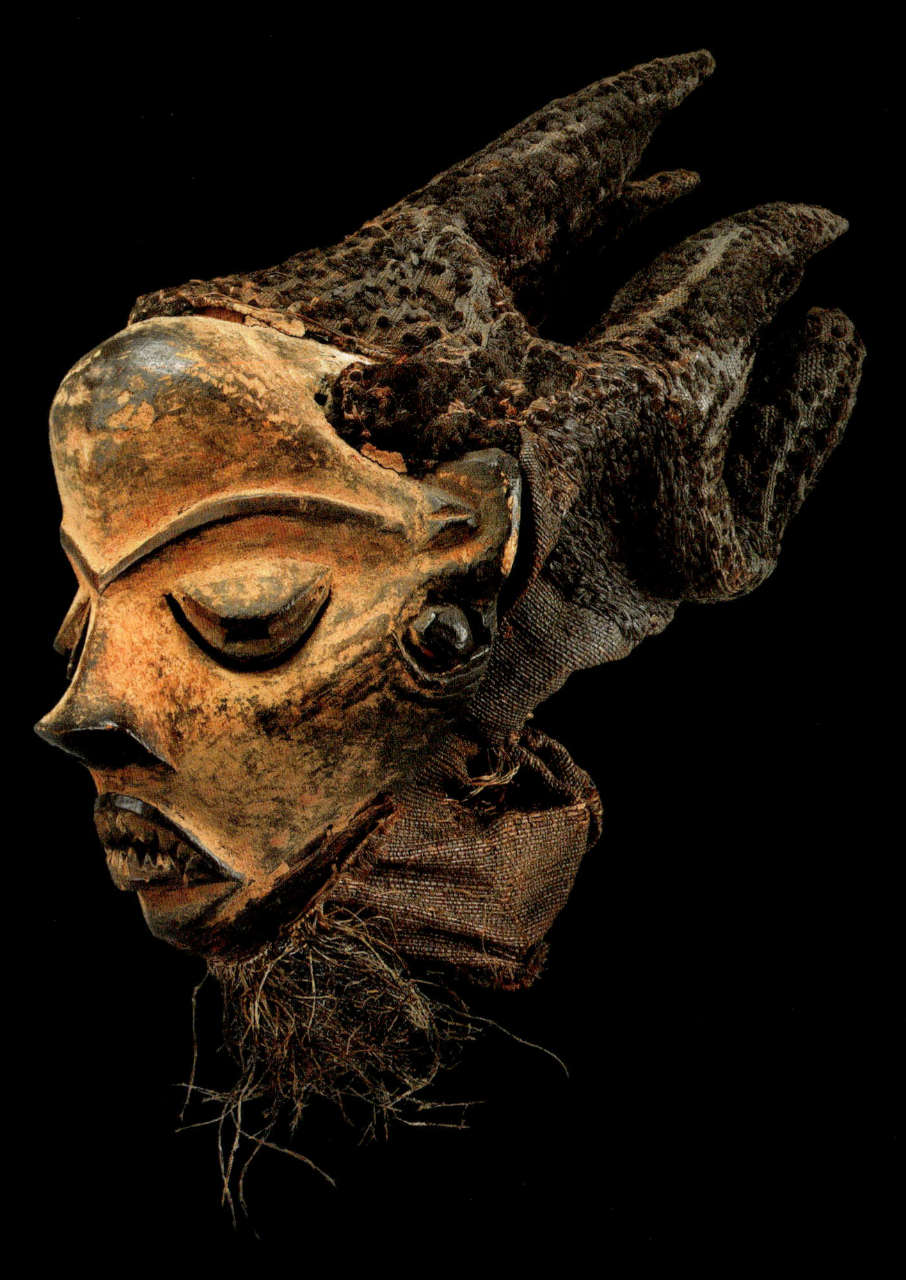

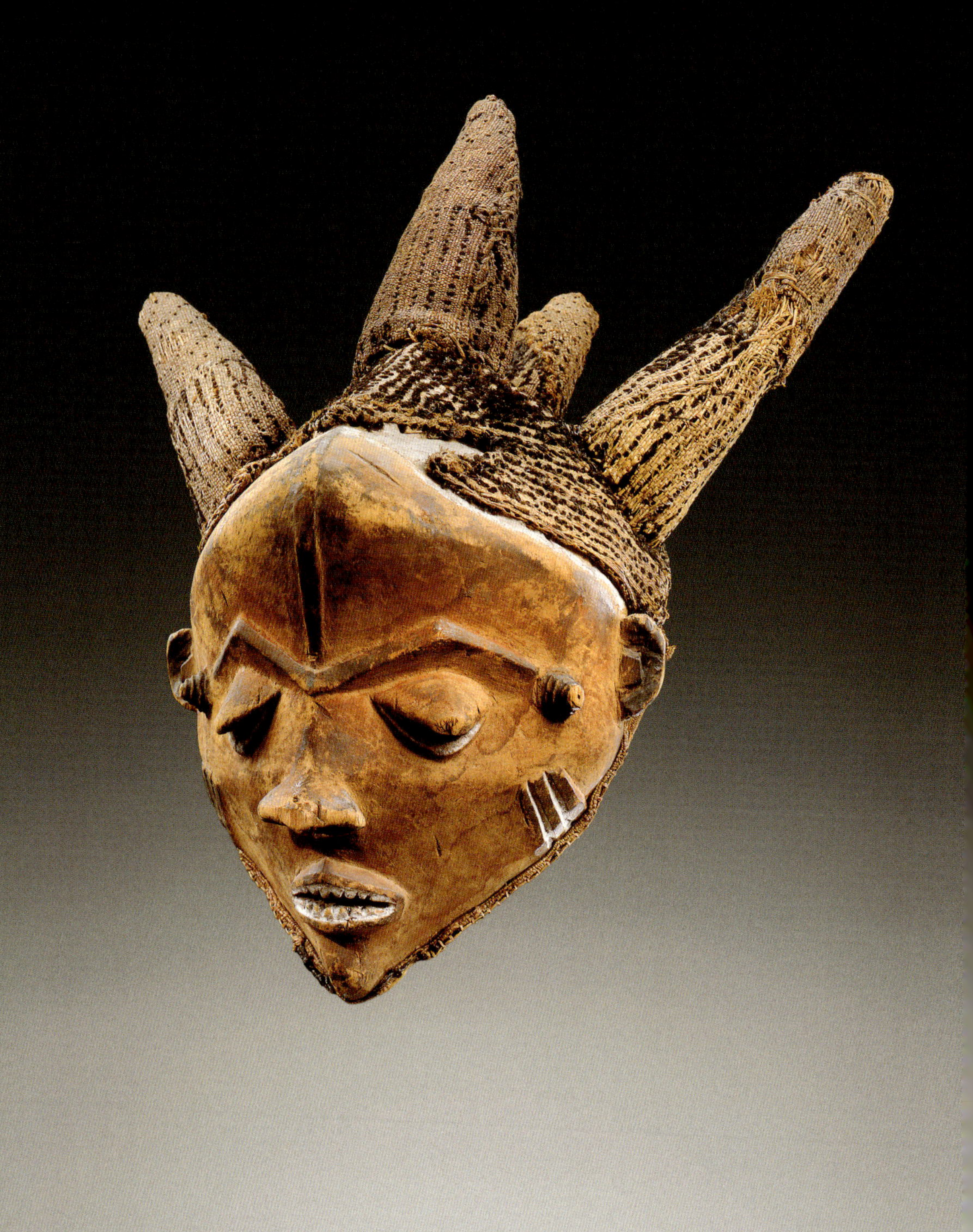

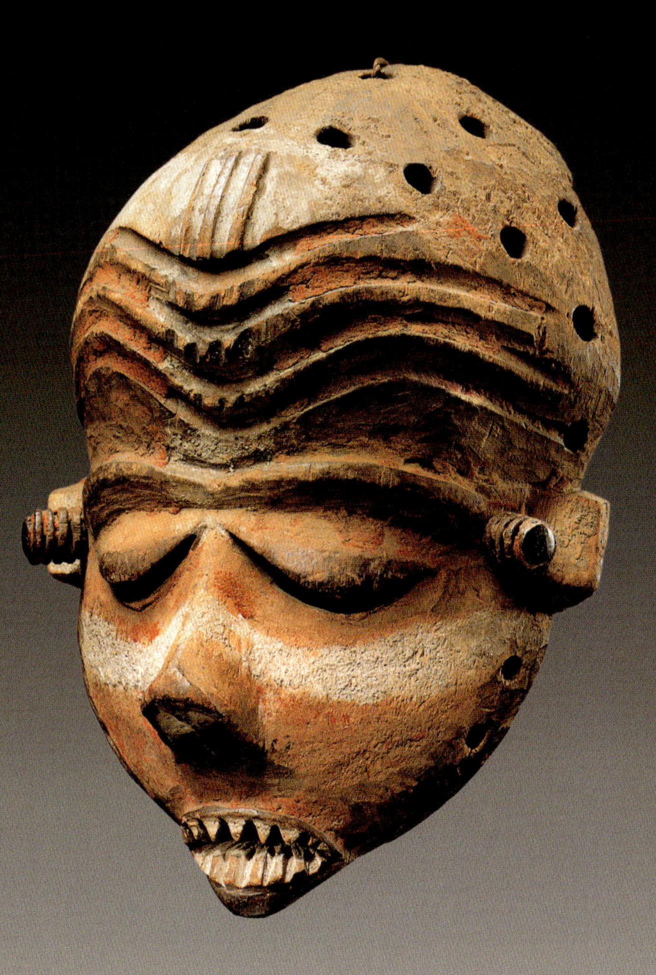

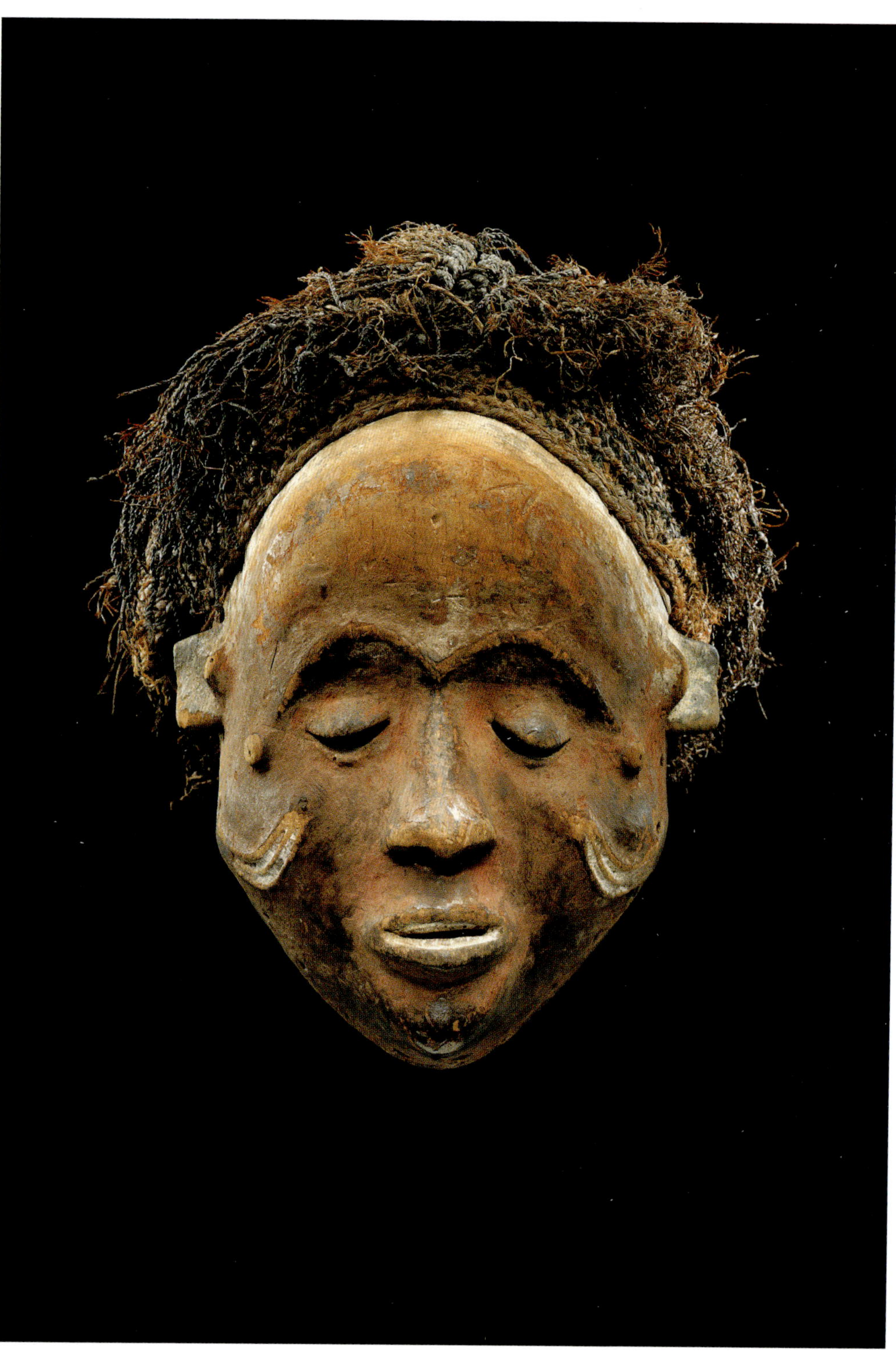

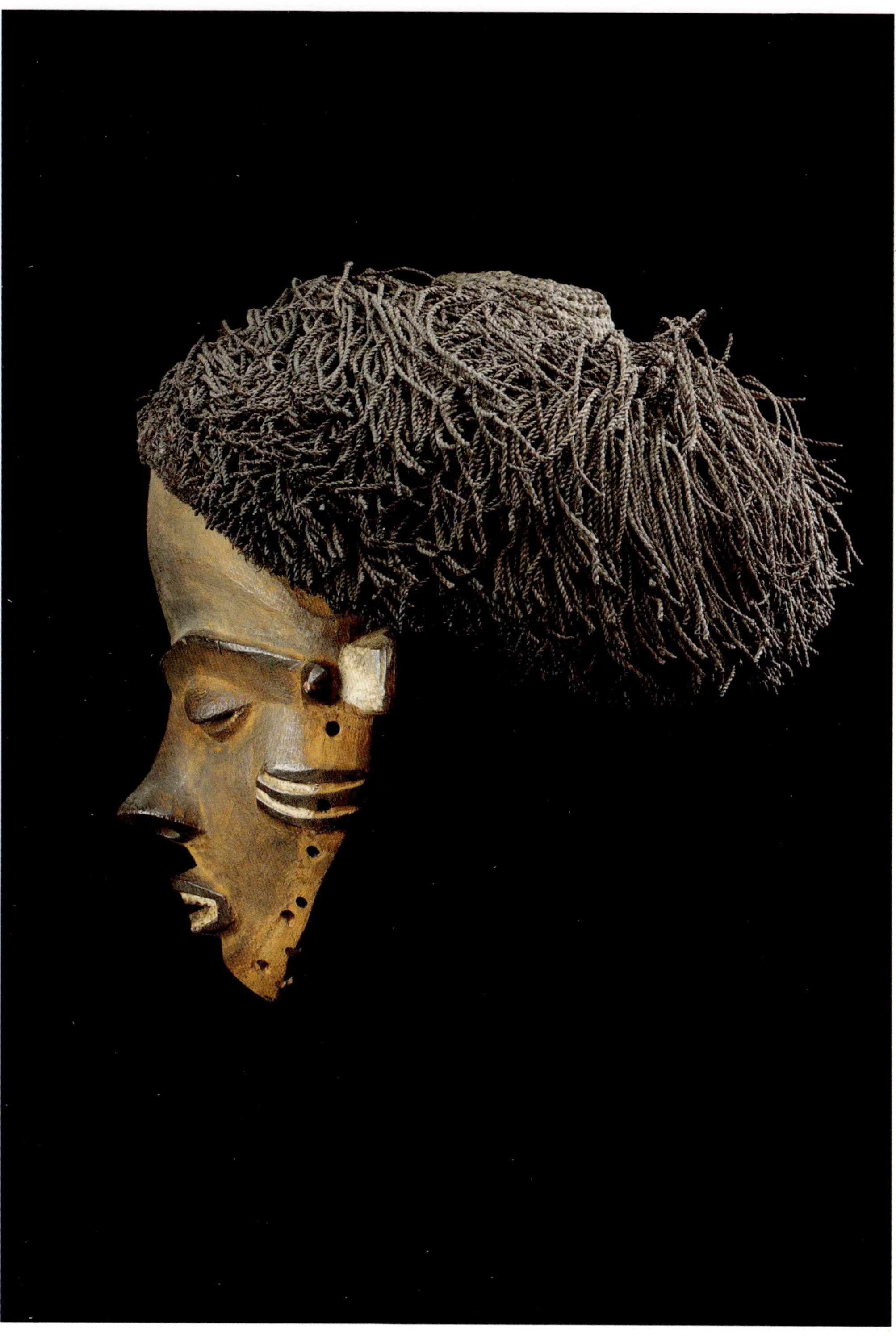

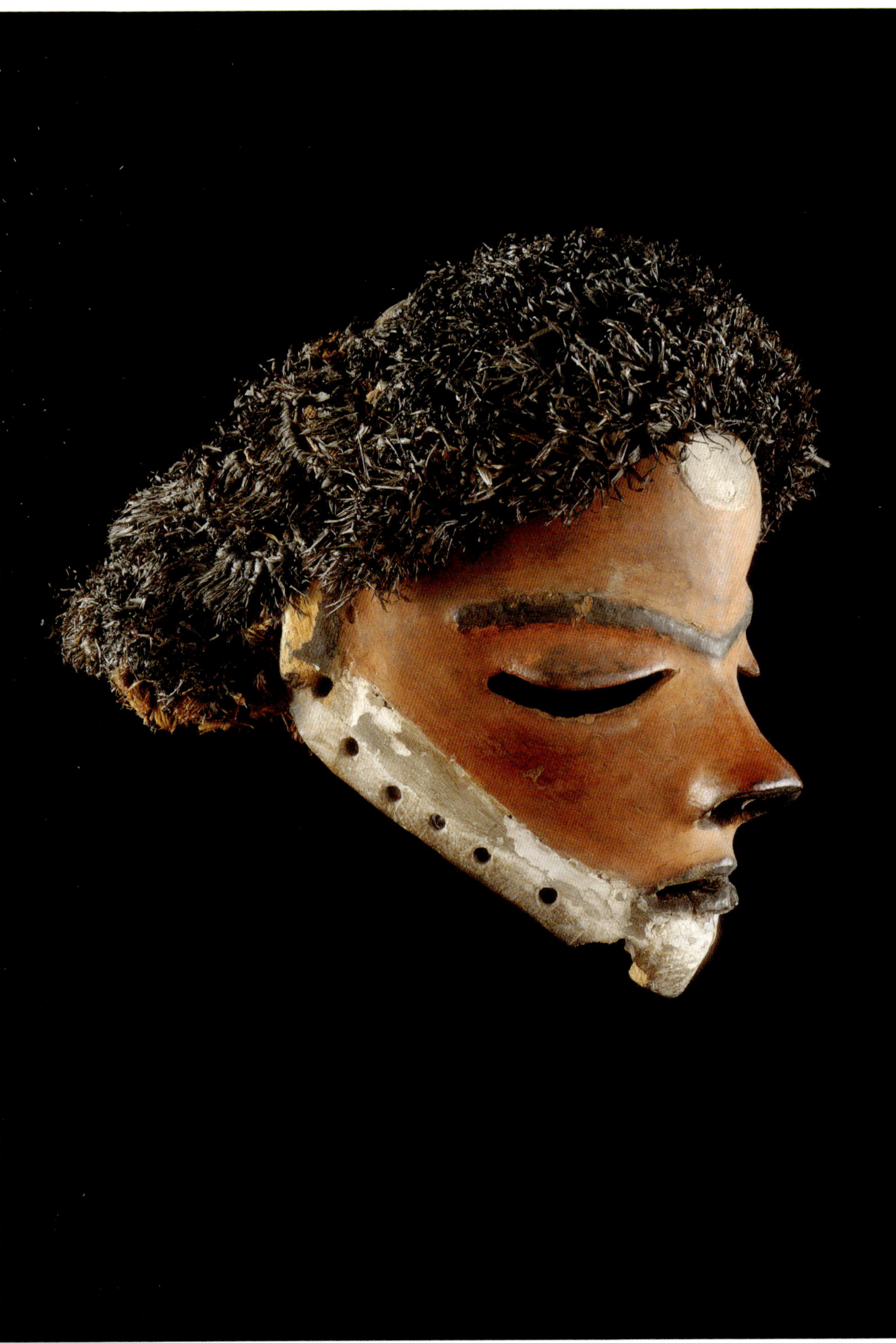

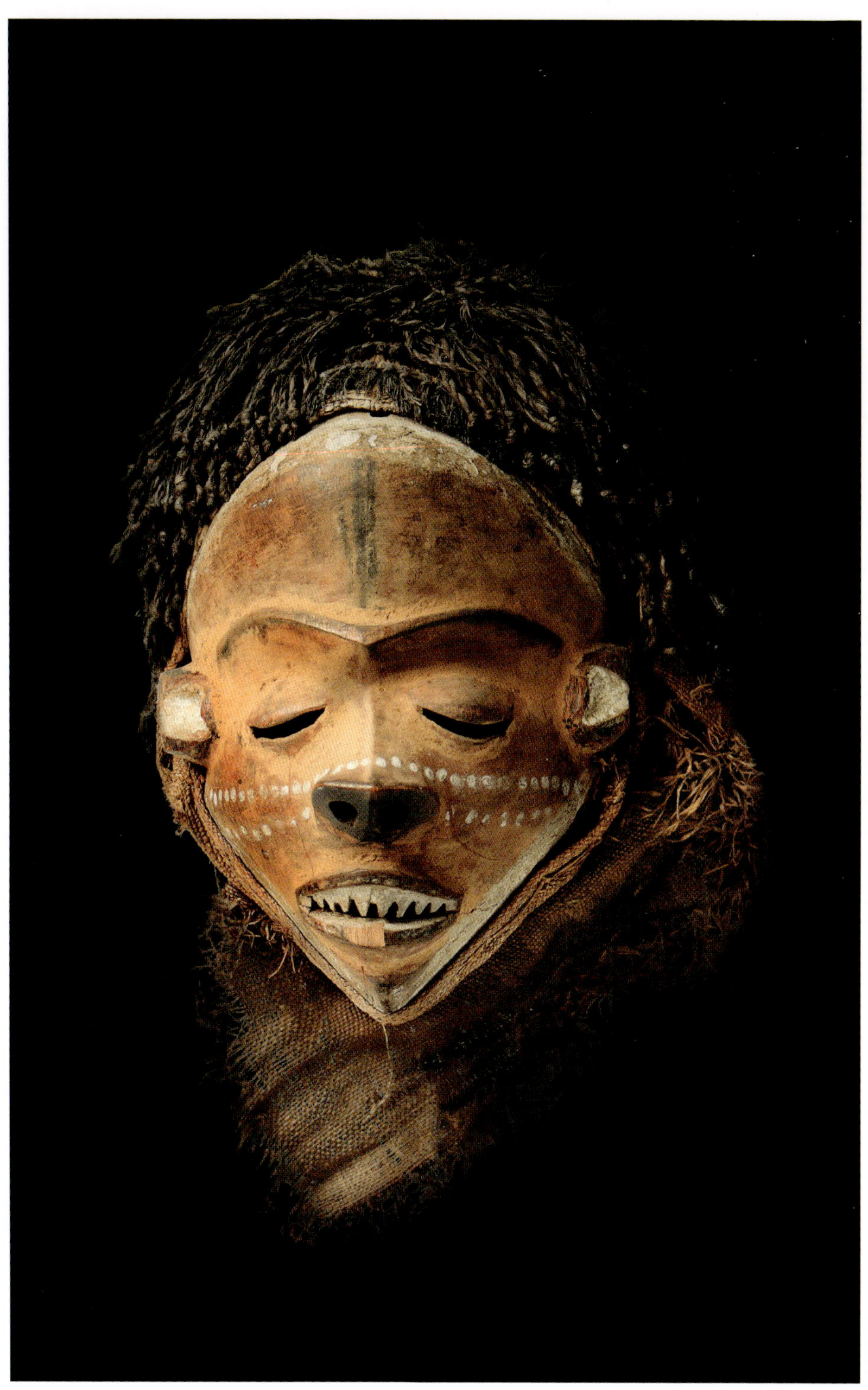

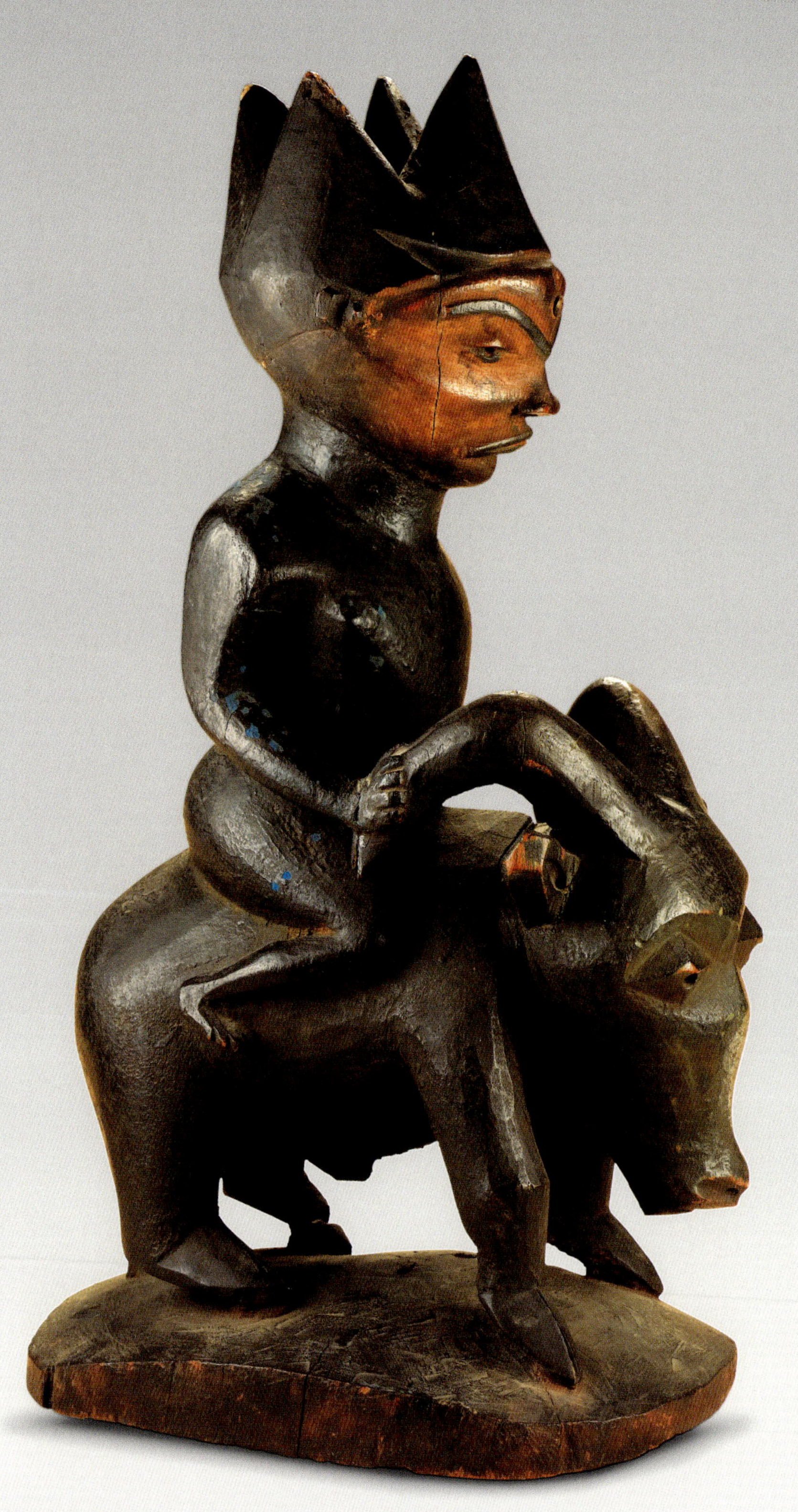

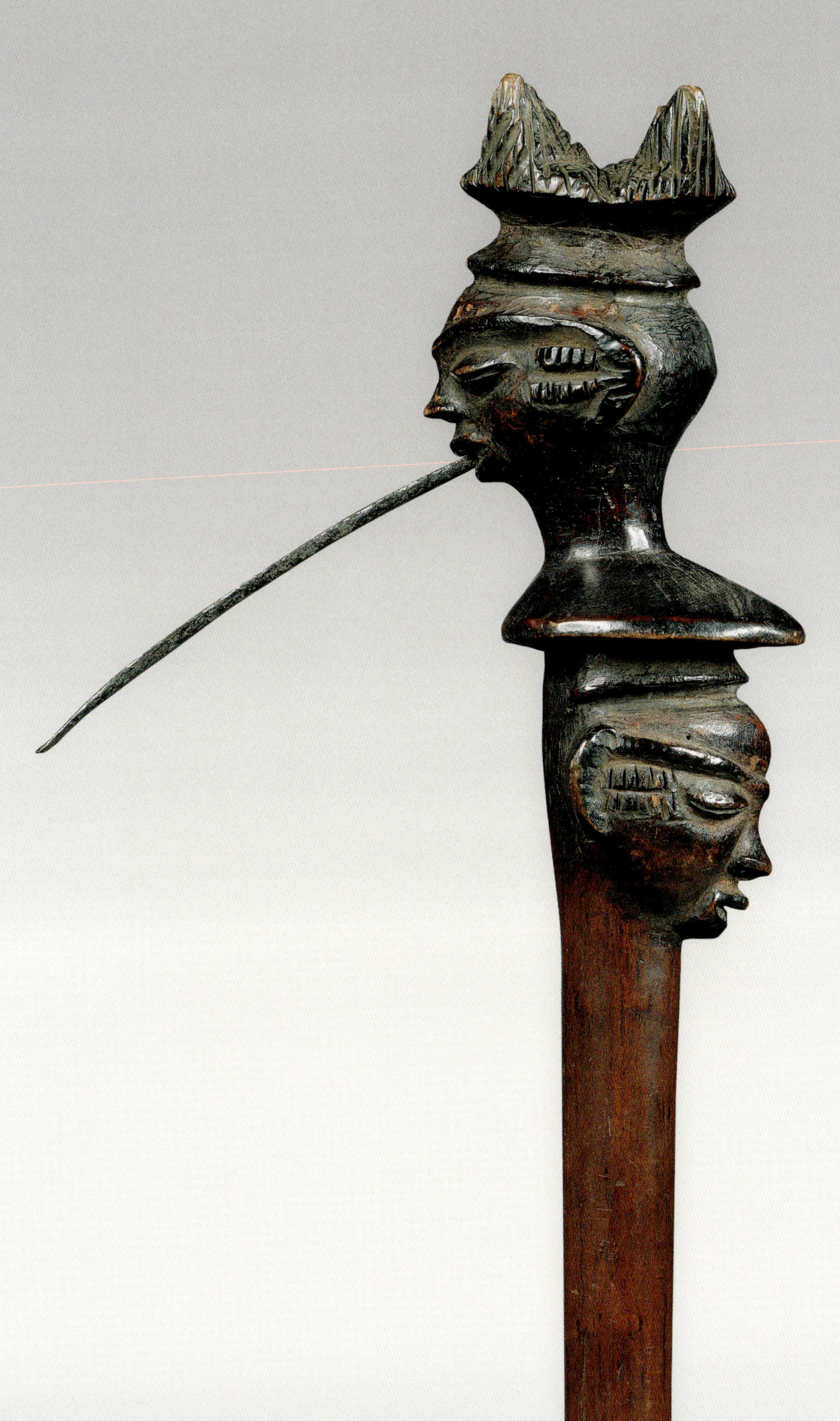

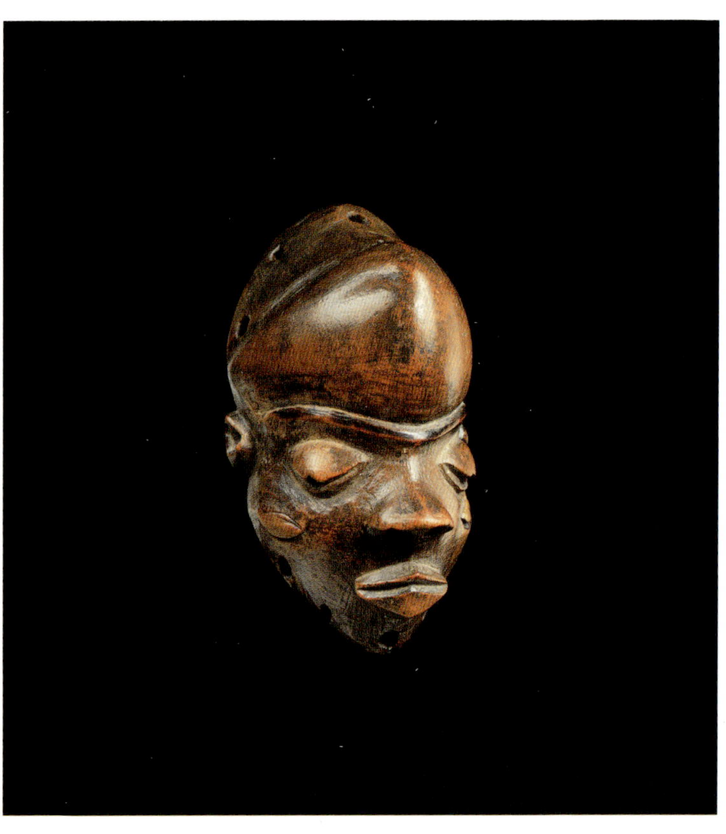

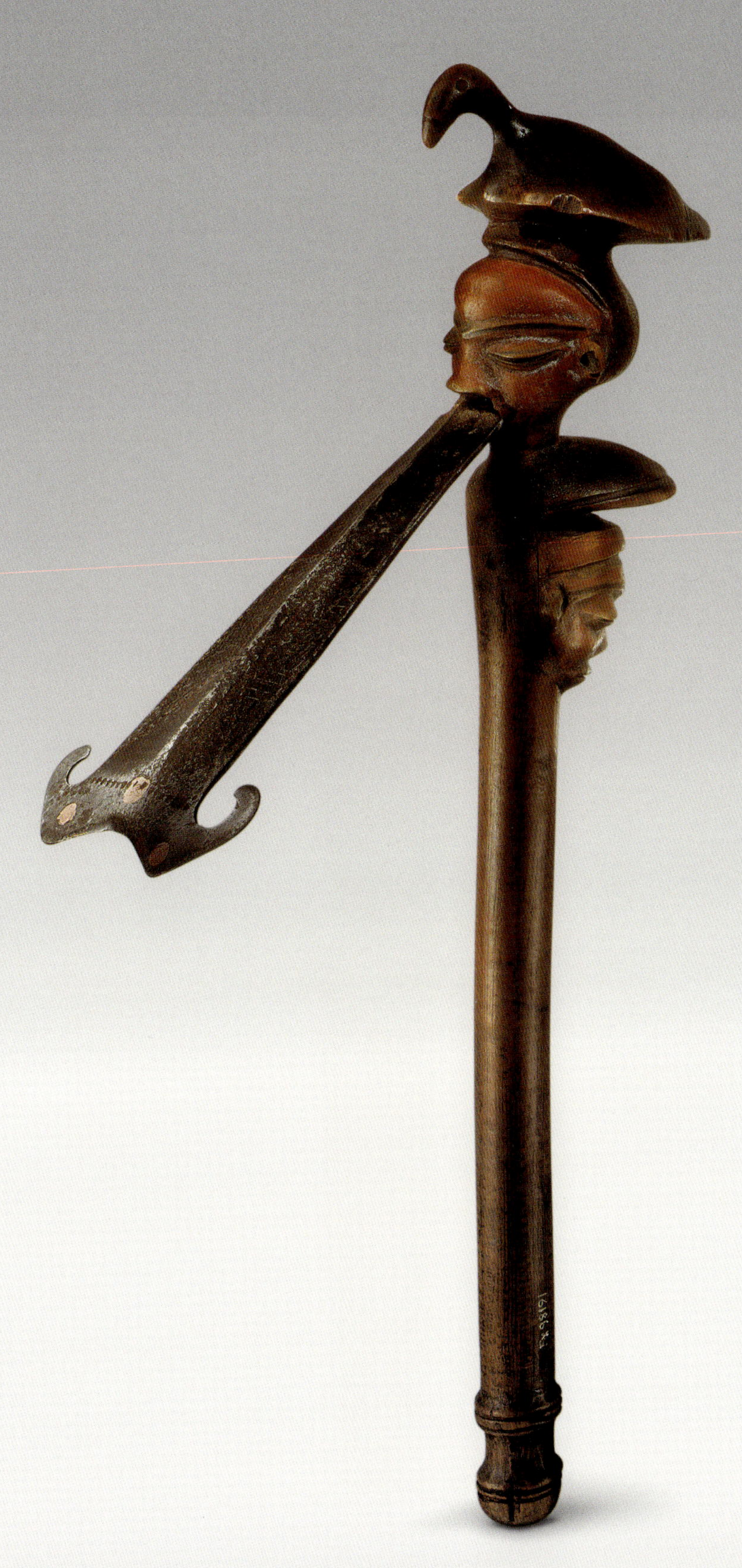

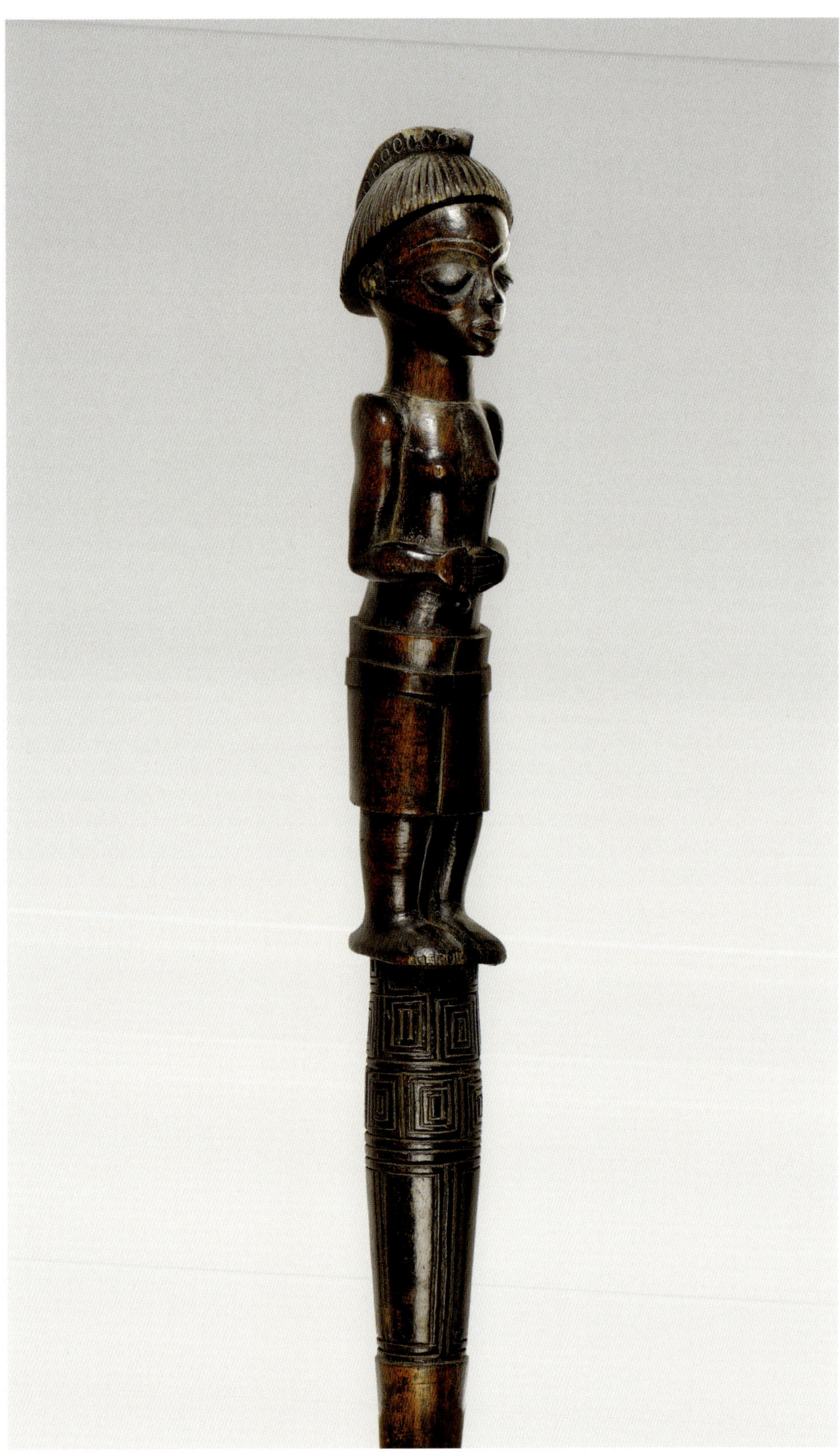

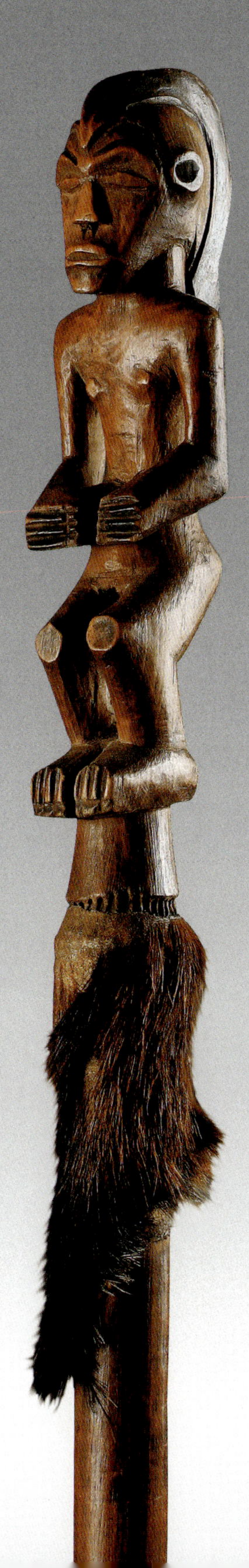

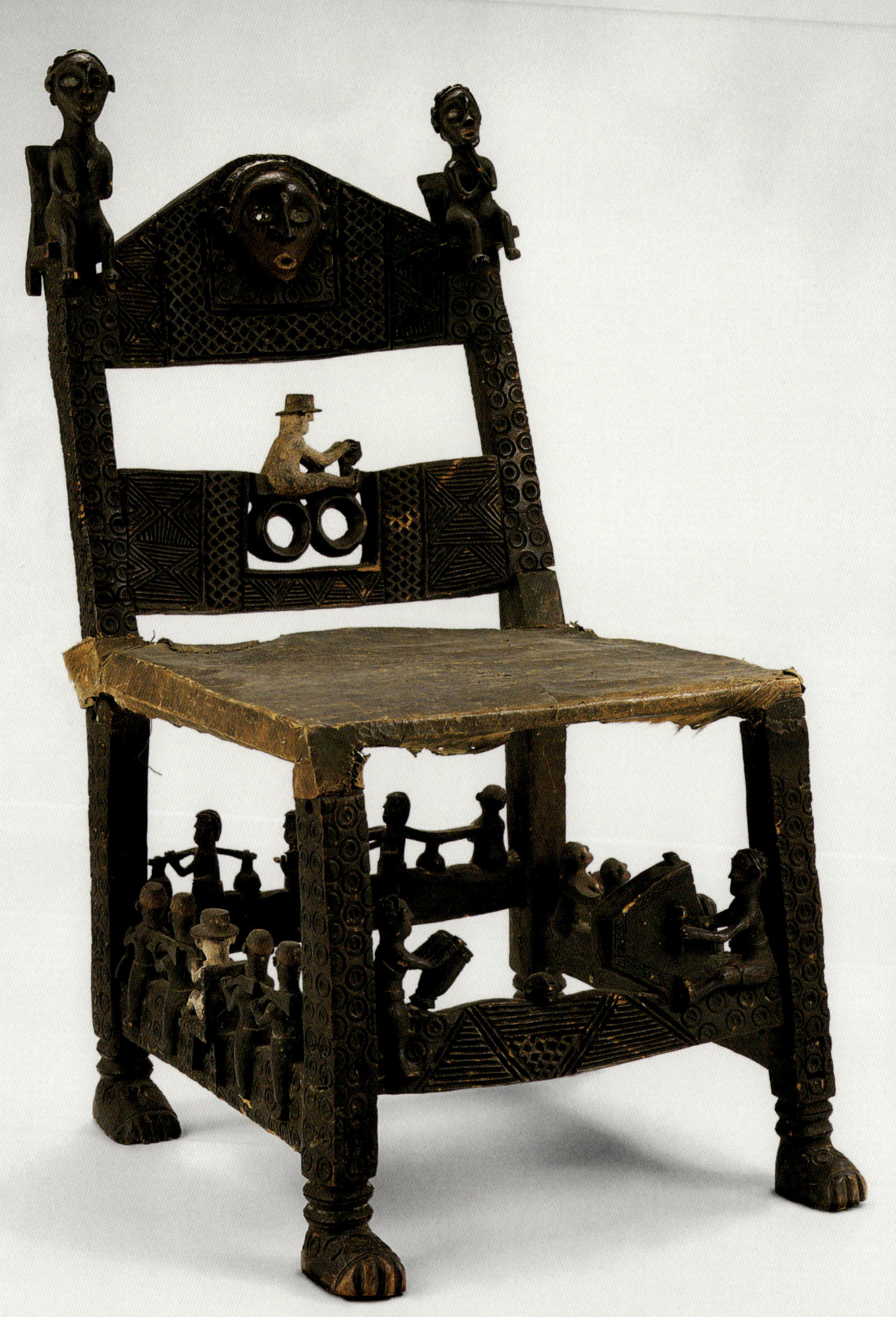

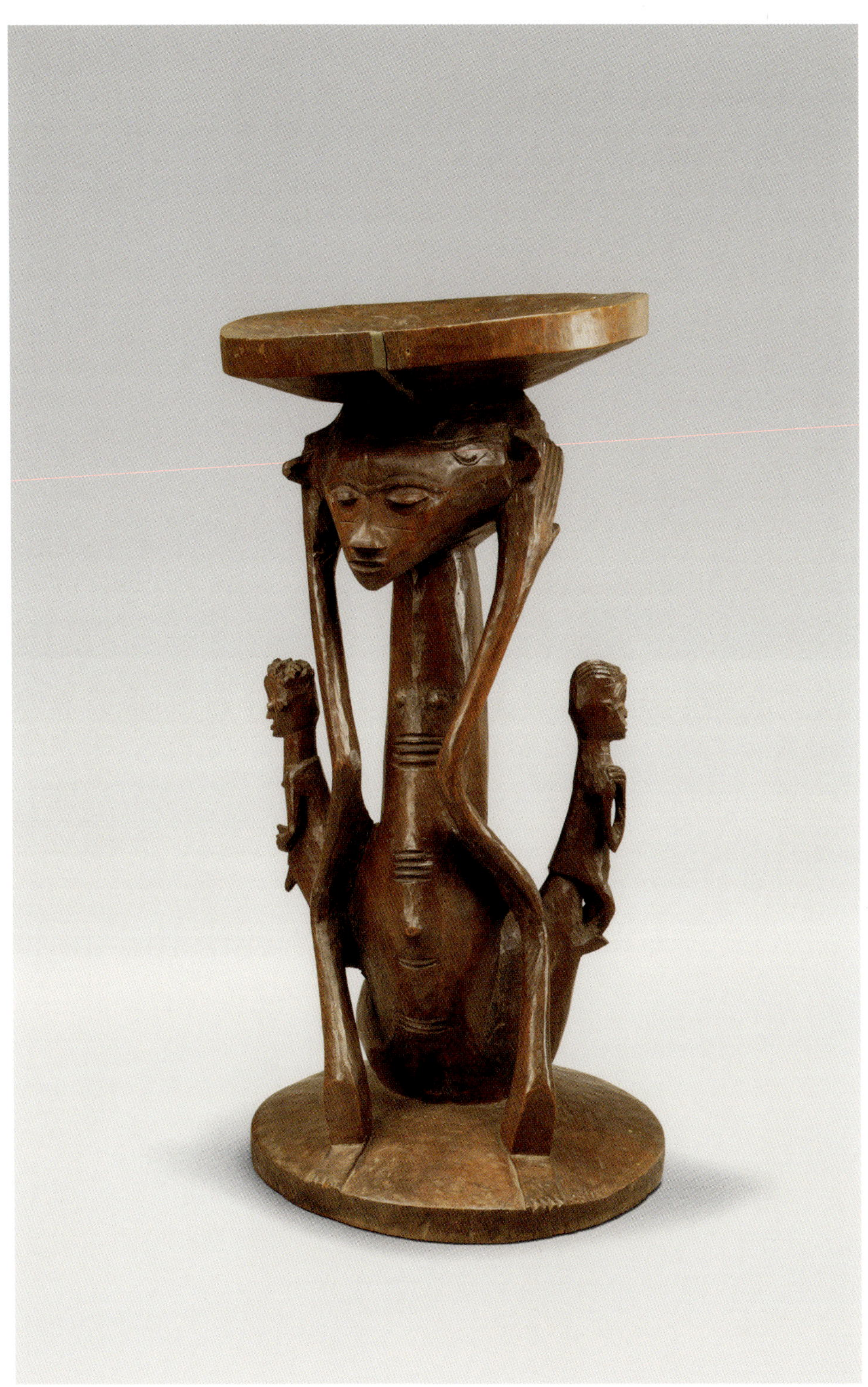

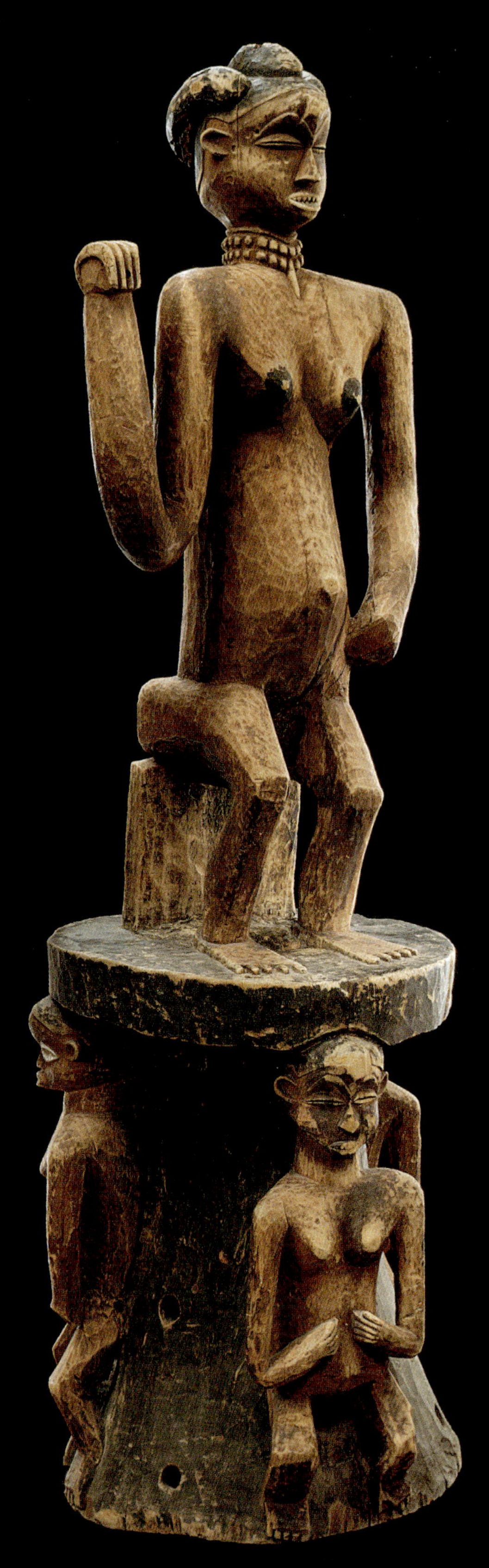

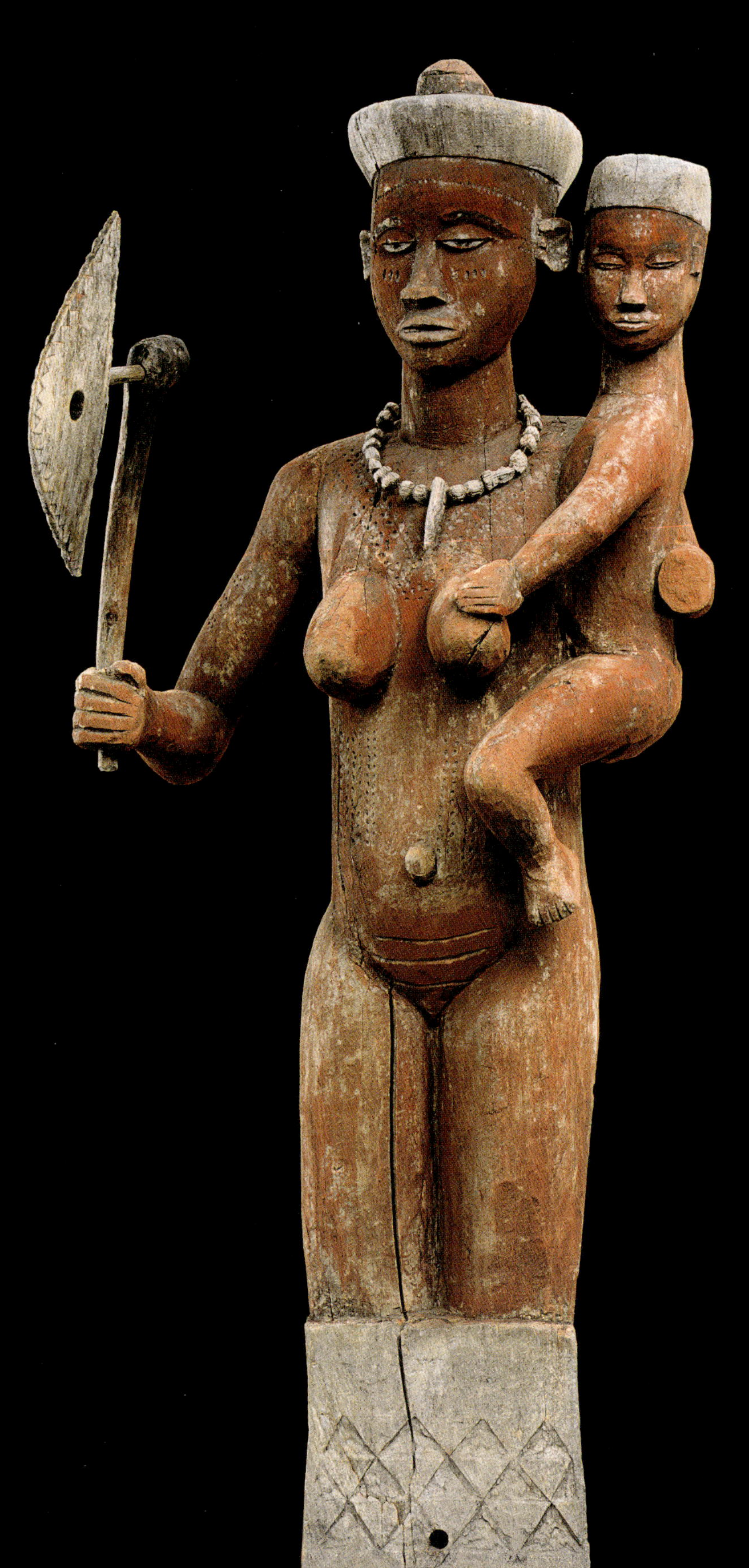

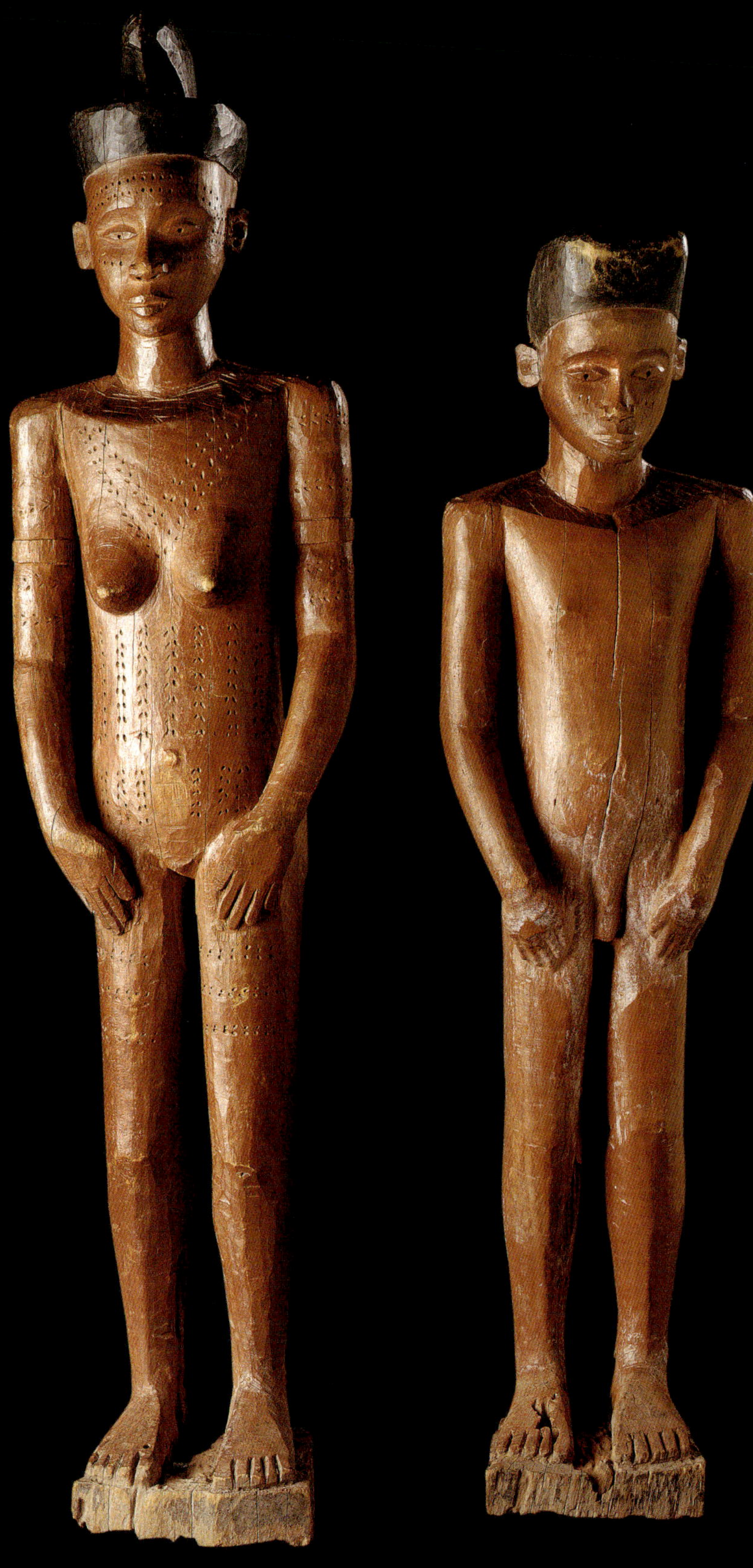

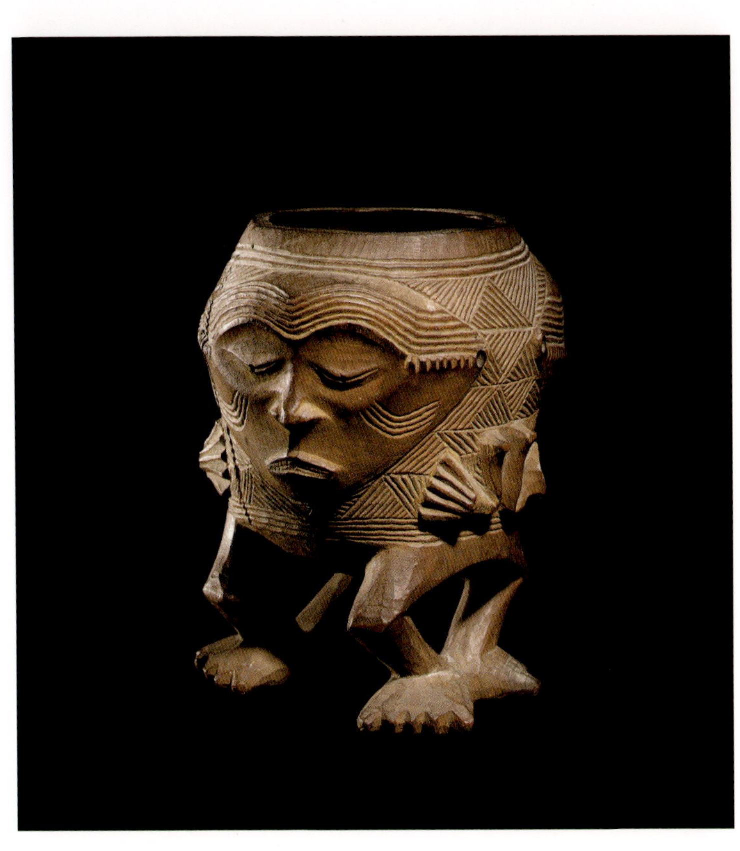

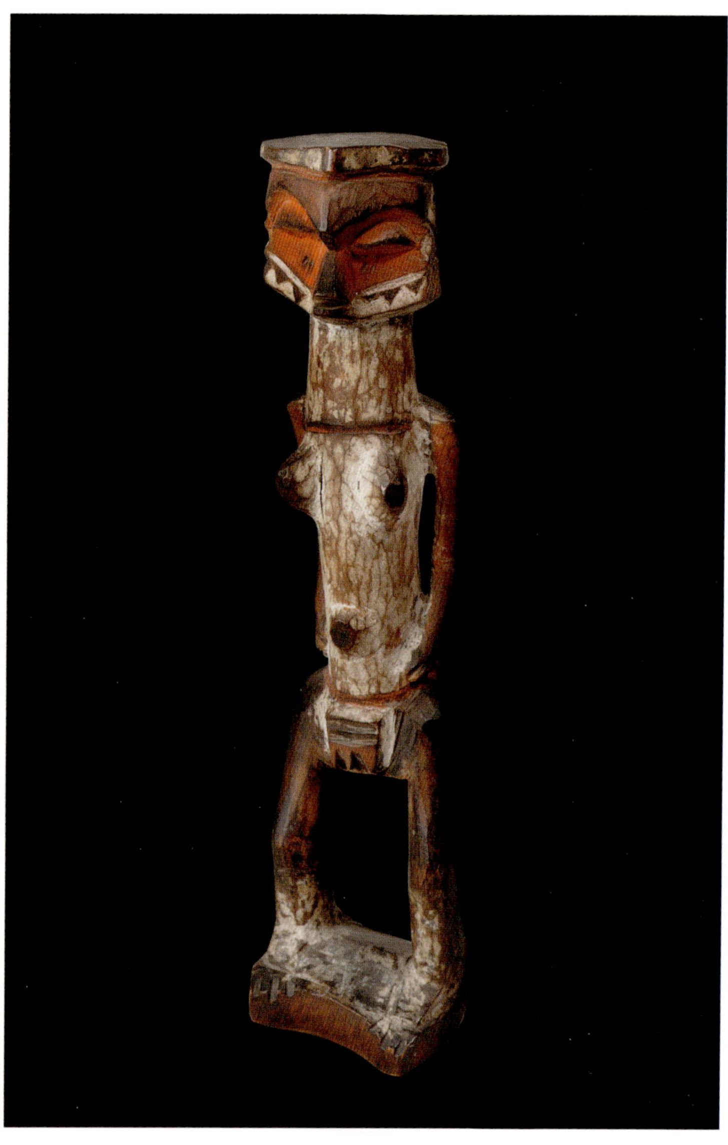

39 - 40

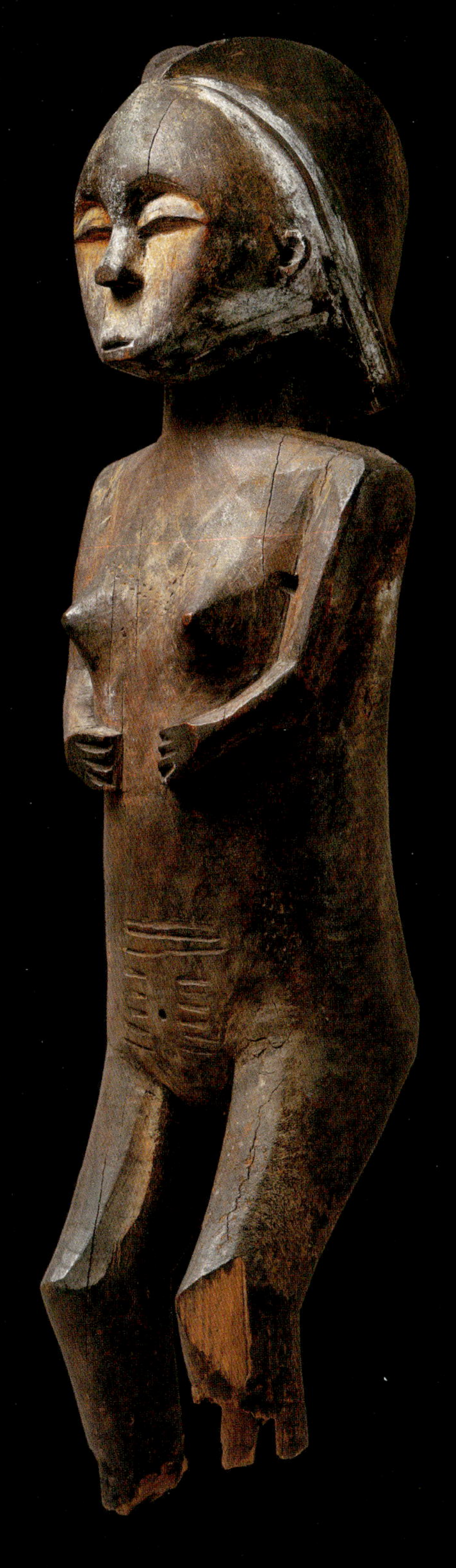

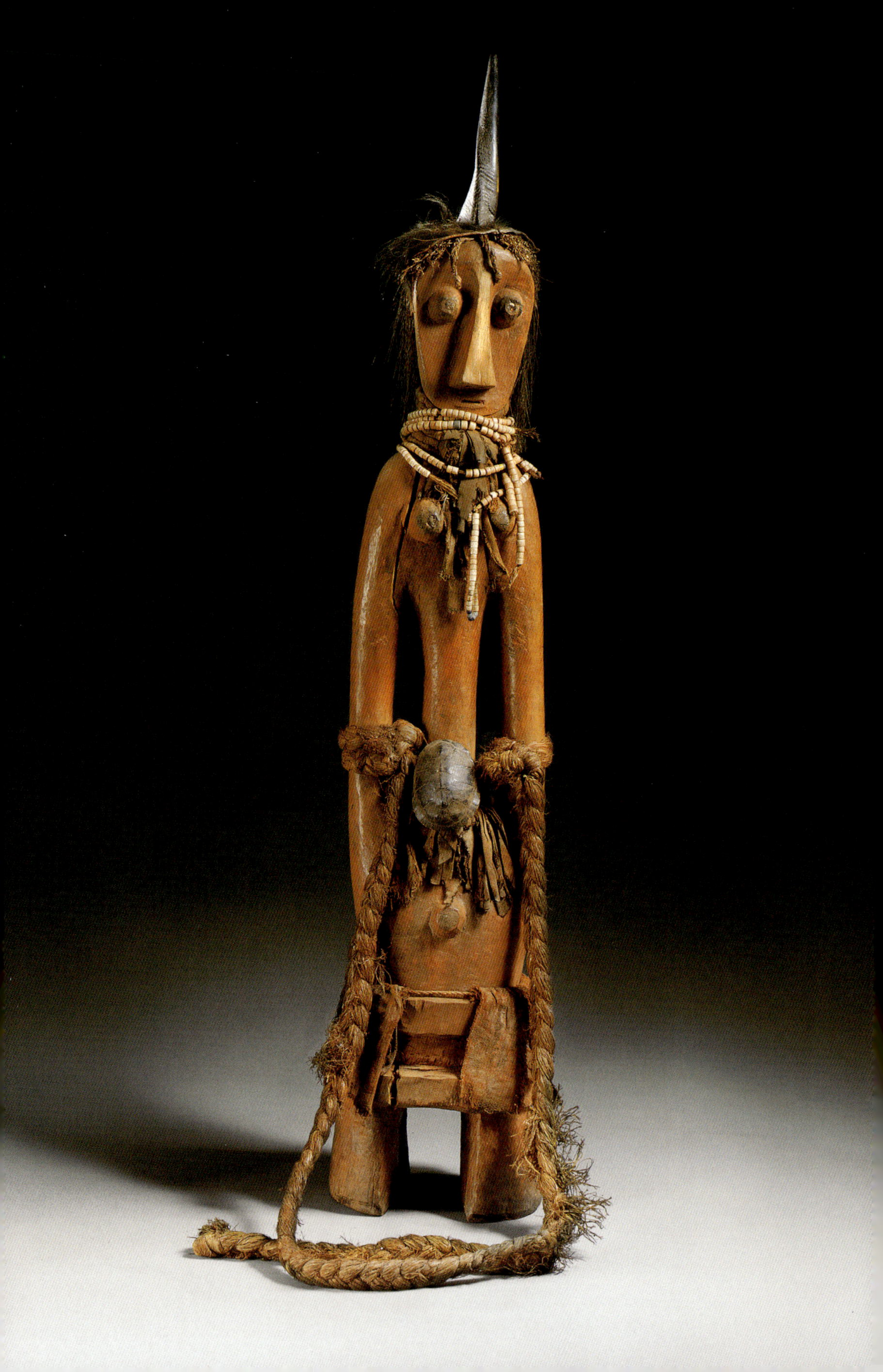

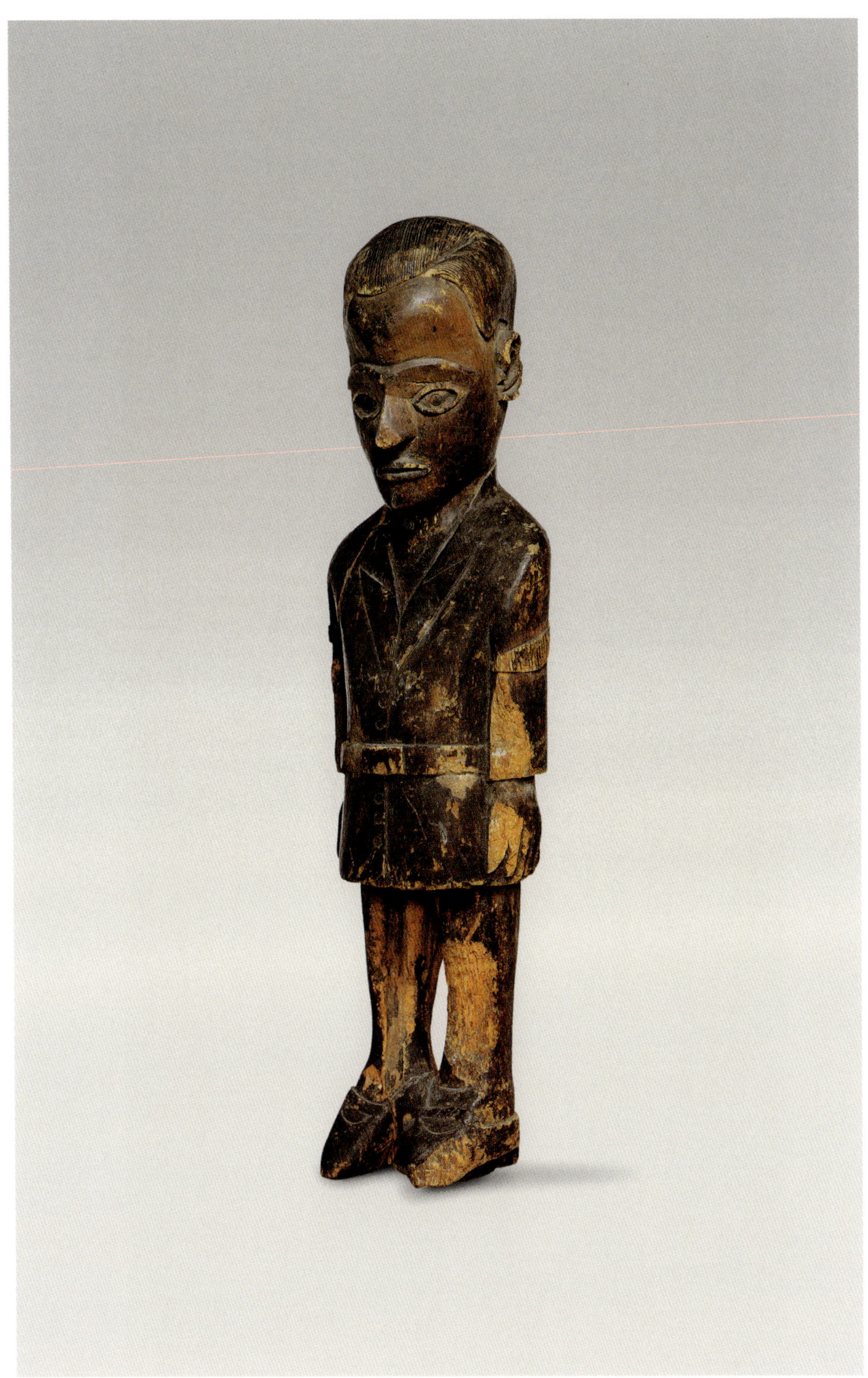

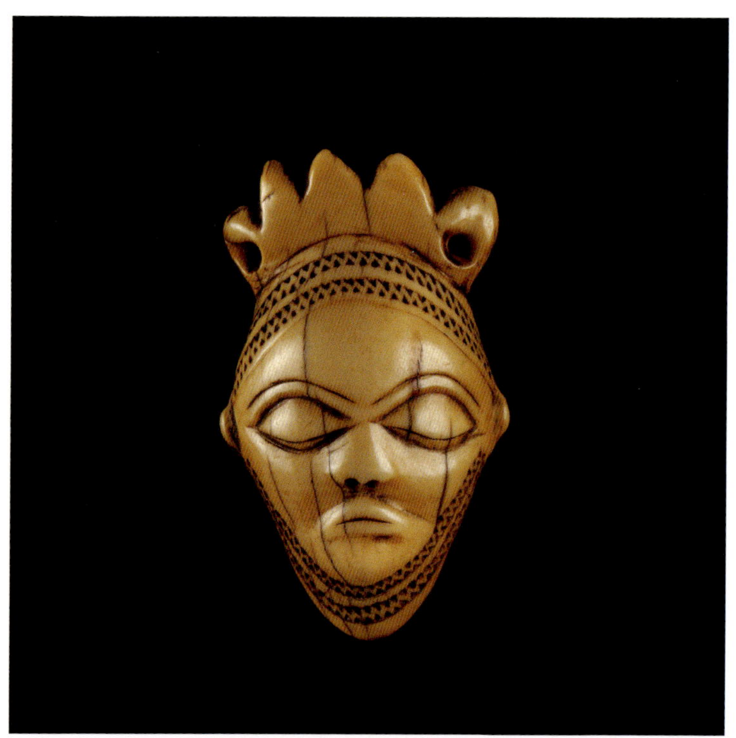

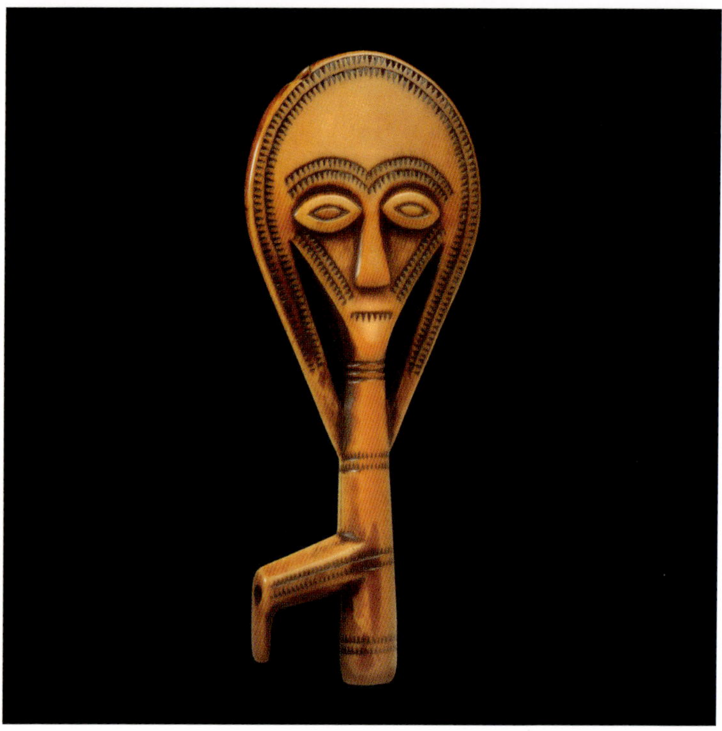

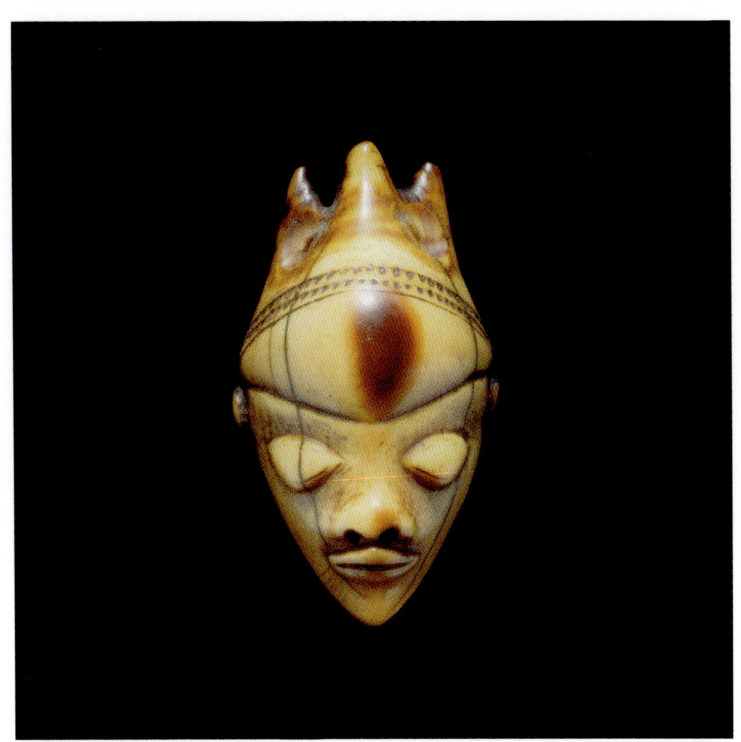

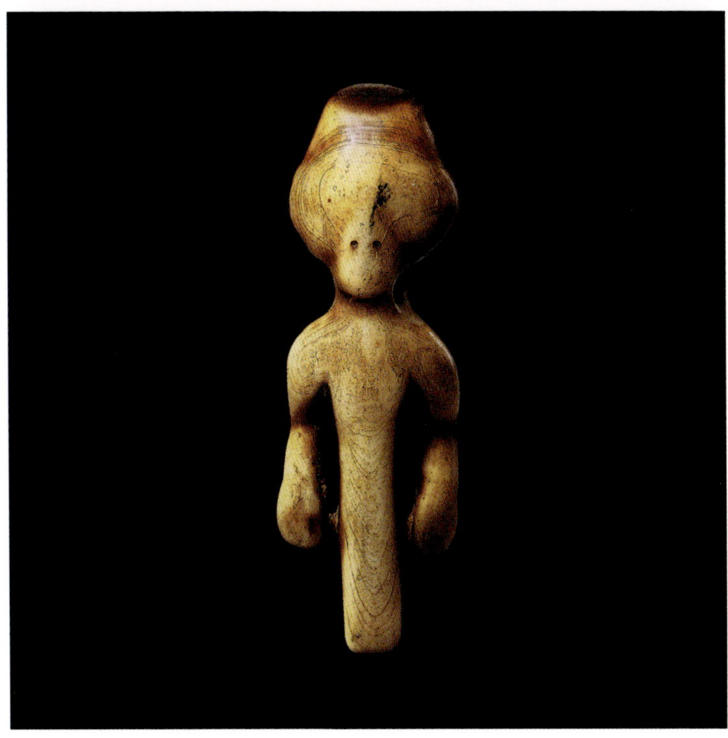

PLATE CAPTIONS

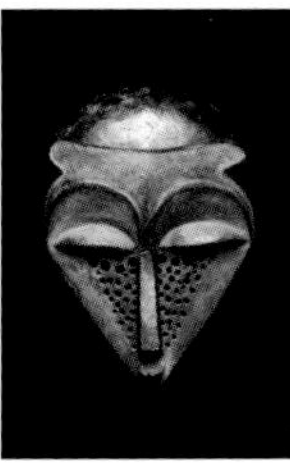

Pl. 1. Kindombolo mask, Eastern
Pende, DRC.
Barbier-Mueller Museum, 1026-25.
Wood, pigments. H.: 20.5 cm.
In this highly geometricised design,
the artist achieves an exquisite tension
between symmetry and asymmetry,
the beautiful and the ugly.
Kindombolo's scars evoke his character
since many argue that survivors
of smallpox lose all respect for
physical danger or social censure.
Called "cruel" because he carries
a whip, Kindombolo (also named
Mabombolo) maintains order
on the dance floor but delights
in outlandish and vulgar surprises.

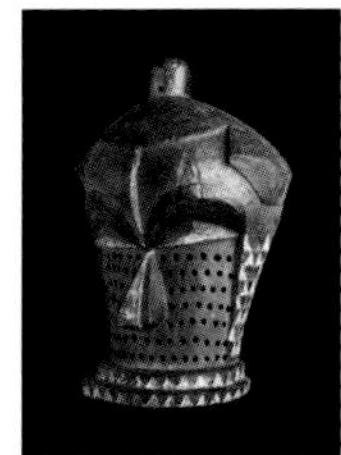

Pl. 2. Kindombolo mask, Eastern
Pende, DRC. San Diego Mesa College.
Wood, pigments. H.: 44.5 cm.
Among the Eastern Pende,
the chief is the owner of all masks.
In this interpretation, the sculptor
emphasises that Kindombolo, however
outrageous, still acts as an agent
of the chief by making references
to Kipoko, "the chief of masks",
in the coiffure, the protruding shelf
below the chin, and the distinctive
diamond-patterning (see pl. 8).

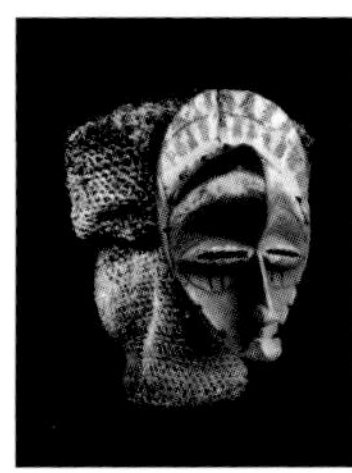

Pl. 3. Pota mask, Eastern Pende, DRC.
Félix Collection.
Wood, raffia, pigments. H.: 23 cm.
Despite the slit eyes, Pota is a forehead
mask, secured in place by the pillbox
hat. It performs with great variety
and often executes manoeuvres
associated with other masks.
In particular, because the dancer
breathes easily and does not tire
so quickly, Pota often takes over duties
from Kipoko so that it is described
as "first minister" among the village
masks.

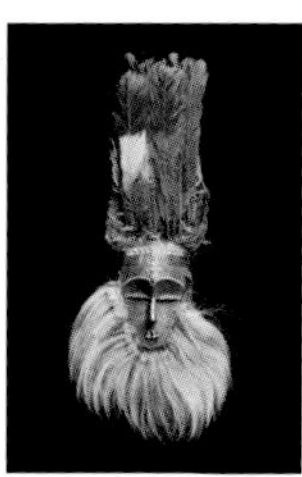

Pl. 4. Munyangi mask, carved by
Kiyova (Luaya-Ndambo village),
Eastern Pende, DRC.
Collected by A. Maesen and registered
in 1953. Royal Museum for Central
Africa, Tervuren, EO 53.74.5395.
Wood (*Vitex madiensis*), feathers,
pigments, headed nails, raffia,
ram's hair. H.: 21 cm, W.: 13 cm.
Munyangi does not represent the great
blue turaco (*Corytheola cristata*)
but shares some of the bird's speed
and agility. The headpiece slopes off
the forehead, leaving eyes and nose
clear, freeing the performer to leap,
twist, and turn.

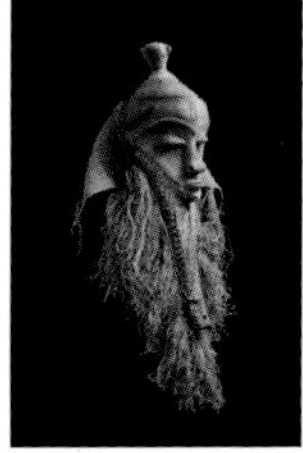

Pl. 5. Kiwoyo mask, Eastern Pende,
DRC. Collected by Hans Himmelheber
in 1938–39. Long-term loan
in Rietberg Museum, Zürich.
Wood, raffia. L.: 52 cm.
Vivid and contrasting colours enhance
visibility as masqueraders cross large
dance arenas. This headdress
(and pl. 6) exceptionally preserve
the true coloration of Pende masks.
The cord dangling from the chin should
be pulled inside so that the dancer
can grip it with his teeth in order
to stabilise the carving on top
of his head, his eyes obscured
by the thick raffia fringe.

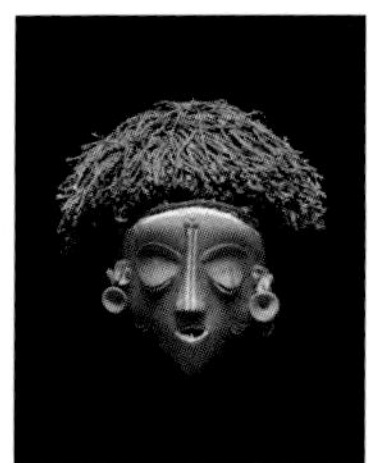

Pl. 6. Kambanda mask, Eastern
Pende, DRC. Collected by Hans
Himmelheber in 1938–39. Long-term
loan in Rietberg Museum, Zürich.
Wood, raffia. H.: 32 cm.
This sculptor has captured the
"bedroom eyes" and plump cheeks
associated with ideal feminine
physiognomy. The separated eyebrows
are in the style of the Central Pende
sculptor Gitshiola Shimuna,
whose work was highly admired
in the mid-20th century. Kambanda
is also called Mbuya ya Mukhetu,
"the mask of the woman".

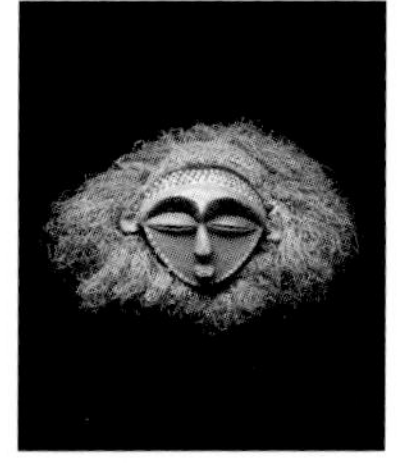

Pl. 7. Panya Ngombe mask, Eastern
Pende, DRC. Collected by Hans
Himmelheber in 1938. Museum für
Völkerkunde, Basel, Inv. III 9508.
Wood, raffia. H.: 30 cm, W.: 38 cm.
Panya Ngombe is a symbol of the right
to host initiations to the men's fraternity
and the right to receive tribute.
Following the rite of circumcision,
Panya Ngombe circulated, collecting
gifts from subordinate chiefs and the
fathers of initiates. Since the colonial
state required circumcision at birth,
the mask itself has become rare,
more often pictured on the door lintel
of the chief's house than performed.
Unlike this example, carefully tailored
to the head of the dancer, the new
masks destined for the international
trade tend to be flat and show
the influence of the door lintels.

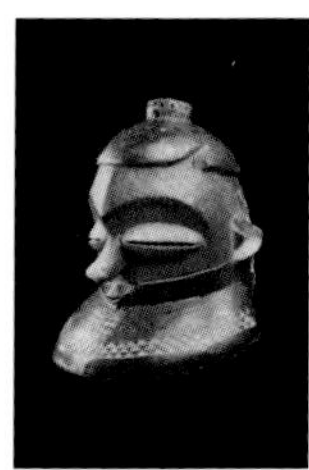

Pl. 8. Kipoko mask, Eastern Pende,
DRC. Collected prior to 1946 by
T. Fourche. Royal Museum for Central
Africa, Tervuren, EO 0.0.43134.
Wood, pigment. H.: 36 cm, W.: 27 cm.
Every chief of every rank has the right
to *Kipoko* (also named *Mukishi wa
Mutsue* or *Mbundju*), which performs
numerous important rituals for the
community. For example, at the end
of his initiation, each boy must grasp
Kipoko by the ears and swallow
a morsel of food placed on his nose
or the shelf underneath in order
to be reintegrated into society.

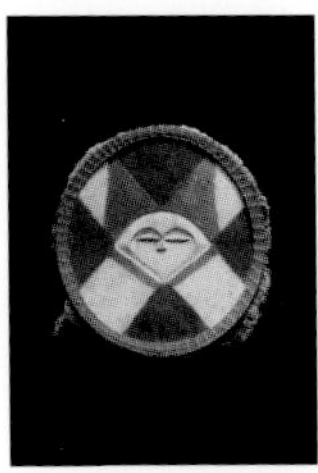

Pl. 9. Gitenga mask, Kwilu Pende,
DRC. Royal Museum for Central
Africa, Tervuren, EO 1975.15.1.
Gift of Comte B. de Grunne.
Wood (*Alstonia congensis*).
W.: 39.4 cm.
The initiation masks of the Kwilu
Pende are called *"minganji."* Gitenga
is unique in this group since the dancer
wears a round, flat disk woven
from basketry materials rather than
a crocheted raffia hood (fig. 2).
This work is one of a small group
carved from wood, despite the
difficulties of carving a flat disk with
an adze. The Minganji are acrobatic
and Gitenga may have been associated
with a cart-wheeling dance evoking
the setting sun.

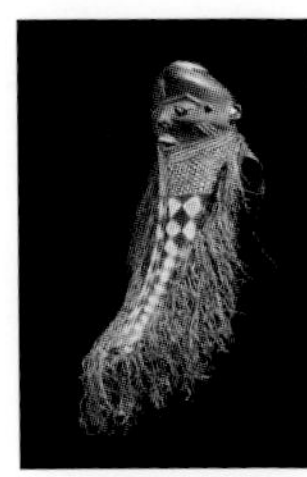

Pl. 10. Giwoyo mask, Central Pende,
DRC. National Museum of African
Art, Smithsonian Institution,
Washington, D.C., Inv. 85-15-5.
Wood, raffia, pigment.
L.: 71, W.: 52, D.: 20 cm.
The photograph is misleading since
the headdress is viewed horizontally
in performance, resting on top
of the head like a baseball cap.
Several Pende specialists explain
that the headdress represents a
cadaver laid out for viewing at a wake.
The arms are placed alongside
the telescoped body, which narrows
and curves up at the end as feet
would, the whole covered by a sheet.
The head joins the body at an obtuse
angle, mimicking the propping up
of the head of the corpse.
The eyes gape half-open in death.

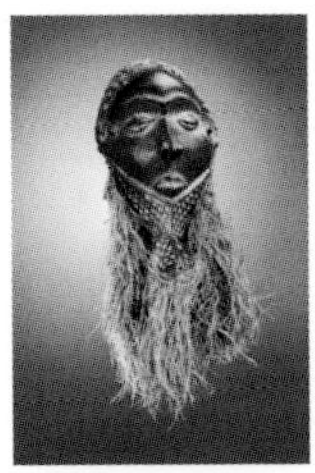

Pl. 11. Muyombo mask, Central
Pende, DRC. Former collection
Isaac Païllès. Private collection.
Courtesy of Entwistle, London.
Wood, raffia, pigment. L.: 50 cm.
This Muyombo is truly a miniaturised
Giwoyo. The sculptor has retained
the obtuse angle at which the head
is propped up from the body
for viewing at a wake and has given
extraordinary expression to the
relaxation of the facial muscles
in death.

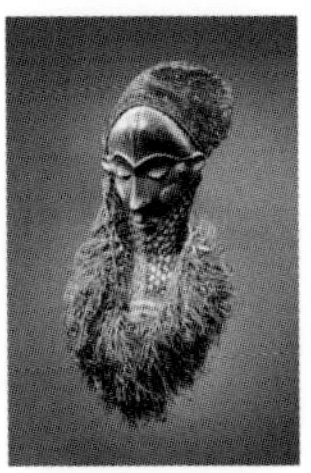

Pl. 12. Muyombo mask, Central
Pende, DRC. Private collection.
Wood, raffia, pigment. L.: 60 cm.
Whereas Giwoyo is carved entirely
from wood, the headdress for
Muyombo sits on the head quite
differently. A soft hat provides a secure
mounting for the smaller headpiece,
which now angles down the forehead,
allowing for prolonged and physically
demanding performances.

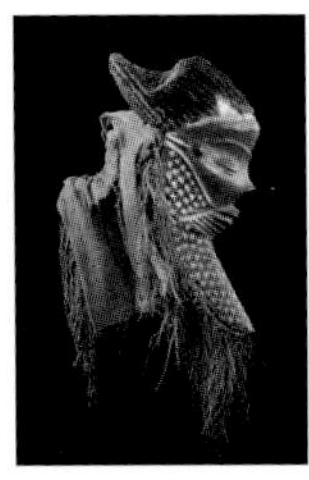

Pl. 13. Muyombo mask, Central
Pende, DRC. Former collection Isaac
Païllès. Collection of Hélène
and Philippe Leloup.
Wood, raffia, pigment. L.: 39 cm.
This lovely work belonged to
a perfectionist. The coiffure is made
from raffia "velvet". The costume
has been skilfully tailored to hug
the back of the neck. The face has
a rosy glow resulting from red bark
paste (*misege*) refreshed for successive
performances.

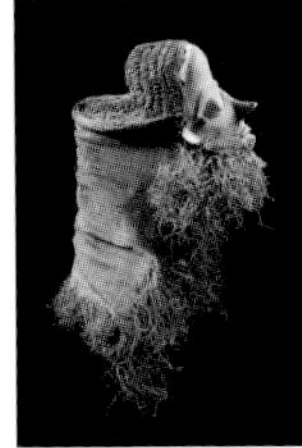

Pl. 14. Pota or Ginjinga mask, Central
Pende, DRC. Ethnological Museum,
Berlin, Inv. III C 19538 (acquired from
Leo Frobenius in 1904).
Wood, palm fibre, pigment.
H.: 22 cm.
One of the oldest documented Pende
sculptures. The photograph accurately
reproduces how the mask would
actually be viewed (largely in profile)
in performance.

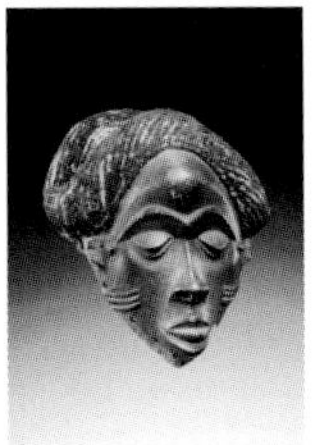

Pl. 15. Pota mask, Central Pende,
DRC. Royal Museum for Central
Africa, Tervuren, EO 1971.43.1.
Former collection J. Walschot.
Wood (*Ricinodendron heudelotii*),
palm fibre. H.: 29 cm, W.: 23 cm.
In *The Broken Ear*, Hergé faithfully
copied this work to illustrate one
of Tintin's comicbook adventures
(Farr 2001: 66). His source was
L'Illustration congolaise (Oct. 1937,
p. 6543), where the mask still bears
a fringe of raffia along the jawline.
The superb patina is the product
of wood polish and removal
of the bright colours appreciated
in performance. The striping
in the coiffure results from shedding
of raffia "velvet".

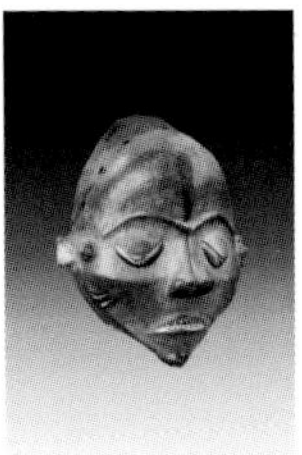

Pl. 16. Unidentified mask, Central
Pende, DRC. Royal Museum for
Central Africa, Tervuren,
EO 0.0.43128
L.: 28,2 cm, W.: 22,2 cm.
The evidence is mounting that in the
19th century most Central Pende masks
were worn sloping off the forehead
rather than covering the face.
In this important transitional work,
the mask has solid, three-dimensional
eyes (showing a good deal of white)
such as one might find on Pota
or Ginjinga, but also slits cut *under*
the eye, indicating that it could be
worn over the face (see also pl. 20).
Later, sculptors developed a more
naturalistic strategy of replacing
the white of the eye with the slit itself
(contrast pl. 17, 18).

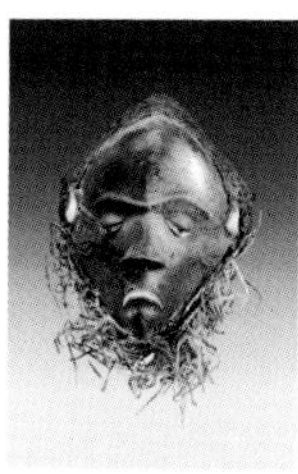

Pl. 17. Mbangu mask, Central Pende,
DRC. British Museum, 1910.4-20-470.
Wood, raffia. H.: 20.2 cm.
A comparison of plates 17 and 18 offers
important art historical documentation.
The work collected by Torday in 1909
indicates that the character of Mbangu
the bewitched was originally conceived
as a forehead mask (without pierced
eyes). However, quickly it became
a face mask, usually associated
with pantomimes. The older sculpture
is recognisable only by the division of
the face into black-and-white whereas
later representations cluster other
traces of chronic illness on one side.

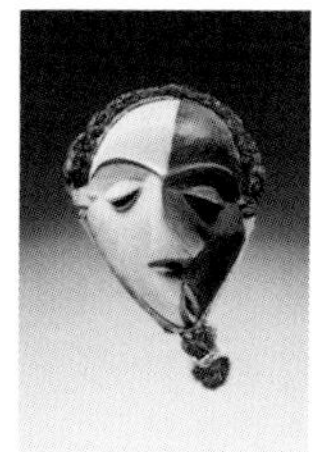

Pl. 18. Mbangu mask, Central Pende,
DRC. Royal Museum for Central
Africa, Tervuren, EO 1959.15.18.
Wood (*Ricinodendron heudeloti*),
raffia. H.: 27 cm, W.: 22 cm.
Although this mask was never danced,
and the coiffure is incomplete,
it is unquestionably one of the finest
Pende sculptures known and testifies
to the vibrancy of artistic life in the late
colonial period. Many Europeans
visited sculptors' ateliers during this
period and one probably purchased
this work before the dancer who
had commissioned it arrived to take
possession.

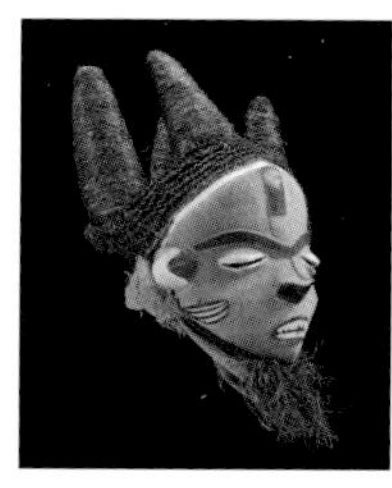

Pl. 19. Fumu (The Chief) mask,
carved by Gabama a Gingungu,
Central Pende, DRC. Royal Museum
for Central Africa, Tervuren,
EO 0.0.32.128.
Wood (*Ricinodendron heudeloti*),
raffia. H.: 22.9 cm (face).
The Central Pende consider Gabama
a Gingungu to be the greatest sculptor
of the 20th century. He also invented
the "face of the chief", which
combines feminine and masculine
features. The coiffure mimics elaborate
hat-like wigs once fashionable among
older men; however, the horns
are plumper and rounder than those
of Pumbu (pl. 20, 21).

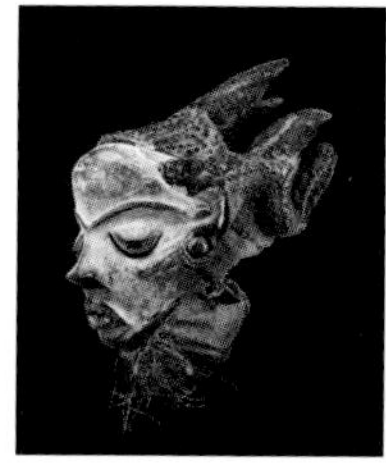

Pl. 20. Pumbu mask, Central Pende,
DRC. British Museum, 1910.4-20.473.
Wood, raffia. H.: 21 cm.
Pumbu represents a paradox:
the imagination of the executioner
by Pende who, historically, lived
in peaceful and decentralised
communities. What would a man look
like who agreed to grapple with
the ghosts of his victims to the end
of his life? In this early interpretation,
the mask's forehead, eyes, and nose
all project outwards with propulsive
energy. The upper lip of *Pumbu*'s large
mouth rises in what Pende interpret
as an expression of anger; he is ready
to bellow with rage.

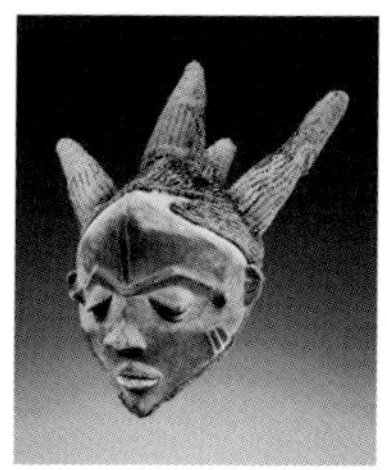

Pl. 21. Pumbu mask, Central Pende,
DRC. Private collection, Belgium.
Wood, raffia, pigments.
H.: 24 cm (face), H.: 49 cm
(with coiffure), W.: 23.5 cm.
The dancers of Pumbu seek the aura
of the leopard: beautiful and yet
terrifying. The masquerader dresses
in sumptuous textiles while
he flourishes a sword. This sculptor
brilliantly captures such contradictions:
the features of the face are small
and delicate and yet rendered with
crisp precision. The forehead protrudes.
The nose flares. The eyebrows, receding
hairline, and chin are all acutely
angled. Most of all, the eyes embody
hyper-male physiognomy as the upper
lids thrust outward into space, pulled
sharply towards the mandibular angle.

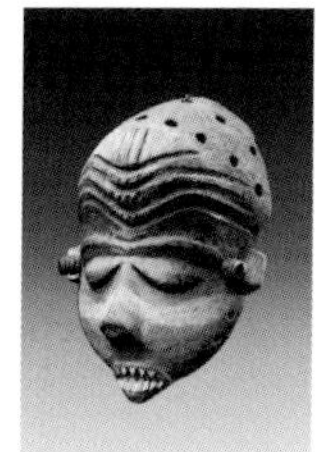

Pl. 22. Unidentified mask, Central
Pende, DRC. Photo Archives
Pierre Loos.
Wood, pigments. H.: 27 cm.
Europeans associate wrinkling
of the brow with anxiety; however,
Pende correlate deep furrowing with
brooding, irascibility, and aggression.
In the late 1920s and 1930s, several
Central Pende sculptors experimented
with giving a naturalistic expression
to this phenomenon by rendering
wrinkles as linear grooves across
the forehead. It is a convention
reserved for frightening personas.

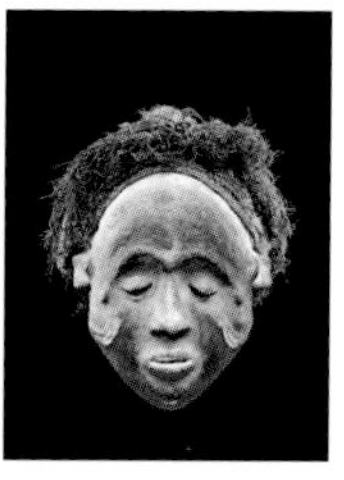

Pl. 23. Female mask, Central Pende,
DRC. Private collection, Belgium.
Wood, raffia, pigments.
H.: 25 cm, W.: 19 cm.
The intricate hairstyles of the female
masks are essential to their beauty.
The work involved in making hundreds
of diminutive braids inflates their prices
and dancers are loathe to part
with them. This sculpture joins Pende
norms on feminine physiognomy
(small, downturned eyes; plump
cheeks; straight mouth) with
an uncanny early naturalism.

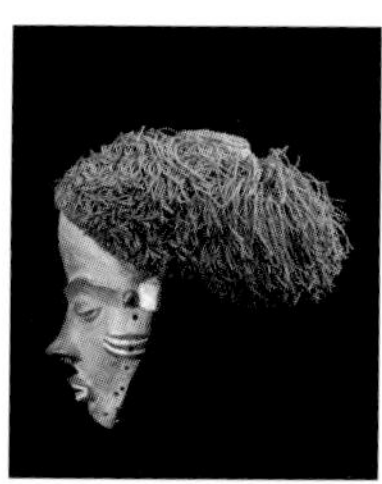

Pl. 24. Female mask (profile), Central
Pende, DRC. Collected in 1934 by
Territorial administrator Maurice
Matton. Ex-Jernander Collection.
Wood, raffia, pigments.
[Dimensions unavailable.]
The epitome of feminine physiognomy,
the mask has a smooth forehead,
softly modelled cheekbones,
and an oval silhouette. In particular,
this artist has captured the "bedroom
eyes" (*zanze*) believed essential
to women's power over men.
The eyes are relatively small in size
and the upper lids curve downwards
to create the impression that they
are nearly closed. The feminine gaze
is classed as the sculptors' greatest
challenge and few succeed.

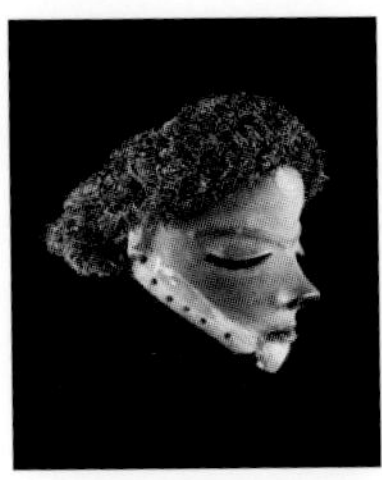

Pl. 25. Nganga Ngombo Mukhetu
(Female Diviner) mask, Central
Pende, DRC. Félix Collection.
Wood, raffia, pigments.
H.: 25 cm, W.: 18.5 cm.
There are many signs that this mask
was well-loved by the dancer who
commissioned it. It fits like a glove
on the face. There is a painstaking
repair below the left ear. Most strikingly,
the smooth and glowing patina is the
result of many applications of red bark
powder mixed with palm oil, refreshed
for each performance. The physiognomy
for the female diviner is more
aggressive than that for other female
representations. She can be recognised
here by the mirror-like flattened oval
of kaolin on the forehead, the broad
band of kaolin along the jawline,
and the unusually large eye-openings.

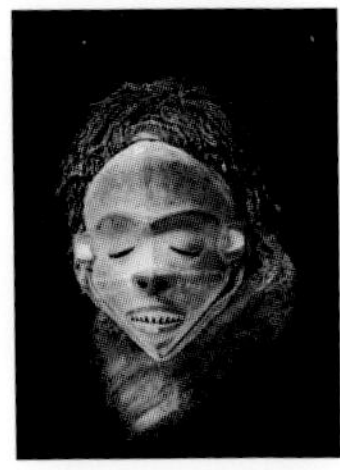

Pl. 26. Nganga Ngombo Mukhetu
(Female Diviner) mask, Central
Pende, DRC. Private collection
Van Damme, Belgium.
Wood, raffia, pigments.
H.: 20 cm, W.: 15.5 cm.
This artist has stressed the androgynous
nature of the female diviner through
the narrow face and distinctly
peanut-shaped silhouette associated
with the representation of the
aggressive male persona. The white
dots underscore her otherworldly
vision. The unusually large mouth,
open ears, upturned nose, and wide
eye slits may also evoke her special
gifts of sensory perception.

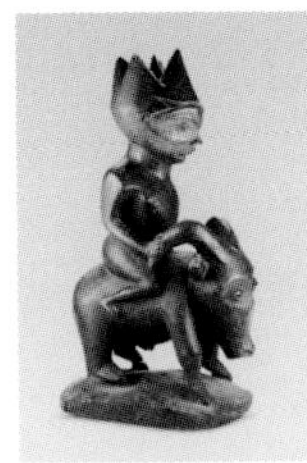

Pl. 27. Mounted figure of a Chief,
Central Pende, DRC. Promised gift
of Barbara and Joseph Goldenberg
to the National Museum of African
Art, Smithsonian Institution,
Washington, D.C.
Wood, pigment.
H.: 57 cm, Diam.: 89 cm.
It is likely that this sculpture depicts
the chief metamorphosing into
a bush buffalo, one of the most feared
of his familiars. The face of the buffalo
conforms to representations in Central
Pende masquerade, including the horns
swiveled backwards.

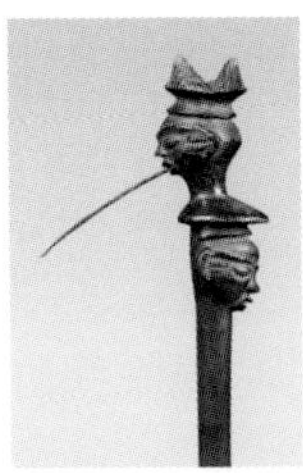

Pl. 28. Chief's ceremonial adze,
Central Pende, DRC. Ethnological
Museum, Berlin, Inv. III C 45038.
Wood, iron. H.: 38.5 cm.
Unlike the sculptor's tool, a ceremonial
adze has a finer blade and figurated
haft. It is associated in folklore
with the chief's propensity for shape
shifting. When he wishes to take
the form of an animal familiar,
he must drive the adze into a tree
in order to be able to regain his own
body afterwards (Gusimana n.d.).
The human forms allude to spirit
workers protecting his person.
Once distributed widely across the
southern savanna (Biebuyck 1985: 76),
the adze has grown uncommon since
Independence, deemed old-fashioned.

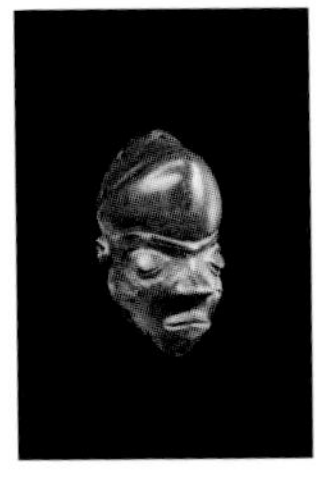

Pl. 29. "Head" attached to *galukoji*
divination instrument, Central Pende,
DRC. Private collection.
Wood. H.: 8.7 cm.
The widow of the diviner who had
commissioned it gave this exquisite
miniature to Léon de Sousberghe,
S.J., in 1953 as a thank-you gift
for employing her son. It originated
in Mbata village, near Ngashi.

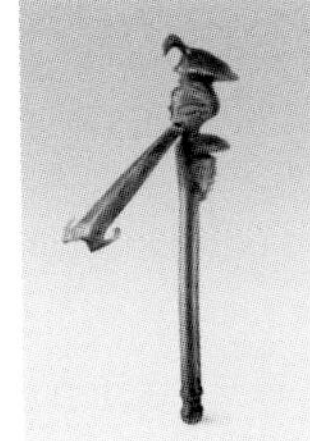

Pl. 30. Chief's Ceremonial Adze,
Central Pende, DRC. Félix collection.
Wood, iron. H.: 44 cm.
This unique work of art blends
two genres. The figurated haft
and the perpendicular angle at which
the blade is attached to the haft
identify a ceremonial adze, which
chiefs wore hooked over their left
shoulder as an emblem of office when
travelling. However, extraordinarily,
the blade itself takes the form
of that used in axes associated
with the investiture of chiefs.
The bird also alludes to the rank
of the chief, since carved birds
were used to identify the ritual
houses of subordinate chiefs among
the Kwilu and Central Pende.

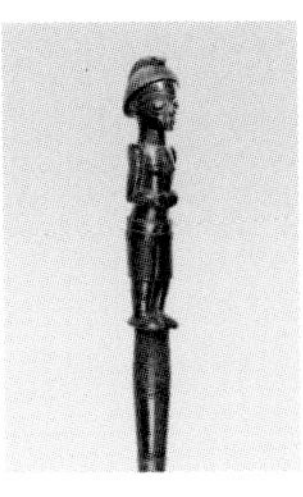

Pl. 31. Judicial staff finial, Kwilu
Pende, DRC. Minneapolis Institute
of Arts, 98.249.3. Gift of The Coudron
Collection – Mr. and Mrs. Albert
J. Coudron.
Wood. H.: 49.5, W.: 5.7 cm.
This work is close in style to several
staffs originating among the Kwilu
Pende, in the south near the Sonde
frontier, although the handling
of the face evokes the form
of Central Pende masks (de Sousberghe
1959: 105, 161, especially fig. 185).
It appears that the staff was cut down
in order to enhance the sculptural
presence of the finial. The seductive
form evokes the abilities of the orator
to weaken his opponents' resolve.

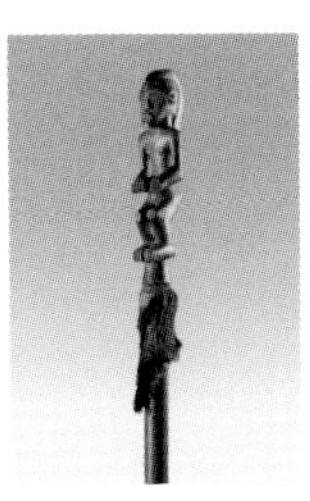

Pl. 32. Judicial staff, Kwilu Pende,
DRC. University of Iowa Museum
of Art, Inv. 1996.249.
Wood. L.: 99 cm.
The taut male form evokes the orator,
alert and ready to act in defense
of family interests.

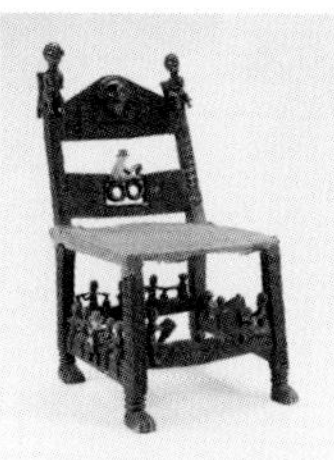

Pl. 33. Sculpted chair, attributed to Muledi (d. 1946) of Mukulu-Nzambi, Kwilu Pende, DRC. Royal Museum for Central Africa, Tervuren, EO 0.0.40078. Registered Jan. 1943. Wood (*Vitex sp.*).
H.: 103 cm, seat 51 x 50 cm.
This chair was photographed by J. Maréchal and published in *L'Illustration congolaise* (1 April 1930, p. 2917) in the portrait of an unnamed Mbuun chief. De Sousberghe identified the chief as Gambunda of Mukulu and mistook the chair (despite different legs) for one that he photographed in the field in 1957 (1959: 113n. 2). The sculptor Muledi enjoyed Mbuun clients and it is possible that Gambunda sold the original chair, which he had commissioned in 1924 from Muledi for his investiture (1959: 26, 116), and replaced it afterwards with another work by the same artist.

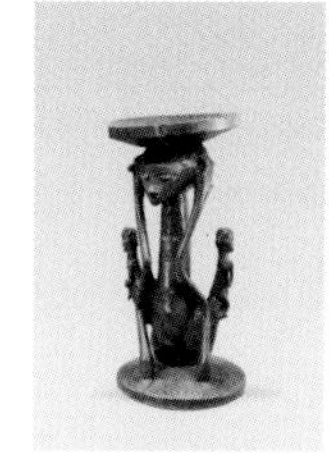

Pl. 34. Caryatid stool, Kwilu Pende, DRC. Registered 1944. Royal Museum for Central Africa, Tervuren, EO 0.0.40324.
Wood (*Vitex congolensis*).
H.: 50 cm. Diam.: 28 cm.
This artist has transformed the caryatid stool by marshalling three figures, looking outwards in different directions, to warn that the chief has vigilant sentinels watching over him. The composition is unprecendented in its dynamism and iconoclastic treatment of the human form.

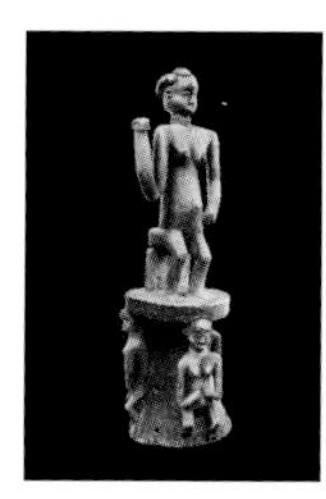

Pl. 35. Rooftop finial, Central Pende, DRC. Royal Museum for Central Africa, Tervuren, EO 0.0.40860.
Wood (*Ceiba pentandra*).
H.: 153 cm, Diam.: 49.6 cm.
Rev. Léon de Sousberghe has traced this work's probable origin, through a former director of the Compagnie du Kasaï, to the Central Pende before 1911 (1954: 78-79; 1959: 162-63). If so, the finial is unique in antiquity and regional provenance.

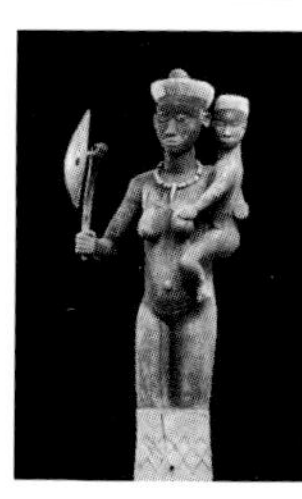

Pl. 36. Rooftop finial, carved by Kaseya Tambwe, Eastern Pende, DRC. Royal Museum for Central Africa, Tervuren, EO 1950.25.1.
Wood, pigments. H.: 110 cm.
Kaseya Tambwe was the artist whom the Eastern Pende considered the most important of the 20th century. He invented the mother and child form for the rooftop finial and pushed Pende art towards greater naturalism.

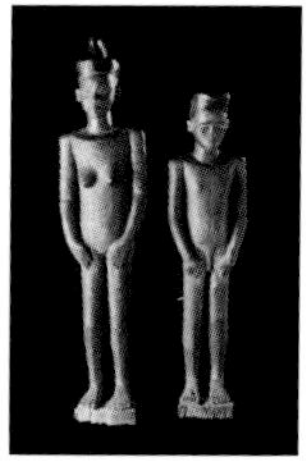

Pl. 37. Door-panel figures (*khenene*), Eastern Pende, DRC.
Private collection.
Wood, pigments. H.: 101.5 cm (male). H.: 121 cm (female).
These two figures were originally attached to panels flanking the door of a chief's house in Kashitu, where they were photographed *in situ* by Nestor Seeuws in 1974. Following the lead of Kaseya Tambwe, all architectural sculptures have been growing increasingly naturalistic. Throughout the course of the 20th century, door panels once carved in low relief are now modelled almost entirely in the round.

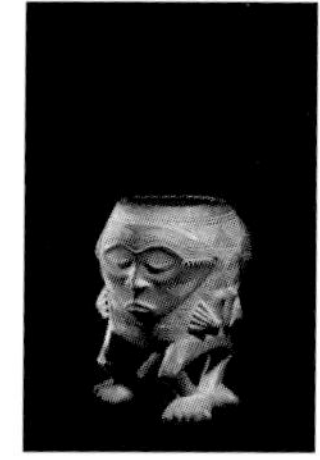

Pl. 38. Drinking Cup, Mpiin, DRC.
Private collection.
Wood. H.: 15 cm.
The most distinctive sculptural creation of the Mpiin is a humorous cup for palm wine, which depicts the drinker as one who keeps his head in his belly. The furrowed brow belongs to the physiognomy of irascibility and warns of the dangers of over-drinking. The cup is beautifully textured to delight the hand. The Mpiin are a Mbuun-speaking enclave who live among the Central Pende. This work testifies to the ease with which artistic styles cross linguistic and ethnic borders as the Mpiin sculptor has appropriated the form of Central Pende masks for a new context.

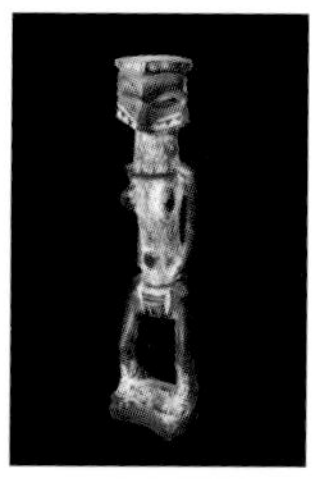

Pl. 39. Female statuette, Eastern Pende, DRC. Private collection, Paris.
Wood, pigments. H.: 31.3 cm.
The sculptor of this rare Eastern Pende statuette was a master of the adze, who transmits some of his own energy to the figure by showing his working process in the faceting of the torso. He reconstructs the body as a vertical cylinder by thickening the neck and treating it as a unit with the torso. The stability of the centre-line creates a fulcrum against which the viewer gauges the asymmetry of the two sides, creating the impression that the body is moving. The eyes turn, the breasts swing apart. From certain angles, she appears to dance. This dynamism attracted the eye of Flemish modernist Armand Vanderlick, who honoured the work in a canvas dated 1936.

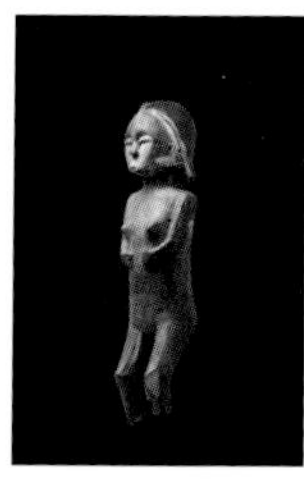

Pl. 40. Kangulungu (female statuette), Kwilu Pende, DRC. Herbert Weiss Collection.
Wood, pigments. H.: 61 cm.
Free-standing sculptures in the round were kept in the inner chamber of the chief's ritual house, where they served as power objects used both to protect and discipline the chief.

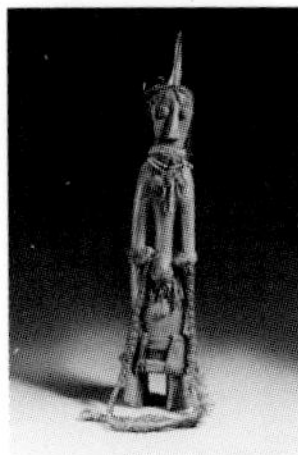

Pl. 41. Njinda power figure, Kwilu Pende, DRC. University of Iowa Museum of Art, Inv. x1986.505, The Stanley Collection.
Wood, tortoise shell, horn, cloth, beads. H.: 102.3 cm.
It is a mistake to think that all power objets draw on the same visual vocabulary. This imposing power object draws on an aesthetic of astonishment and terror. It was used during the Pende Rebellion of 1931.

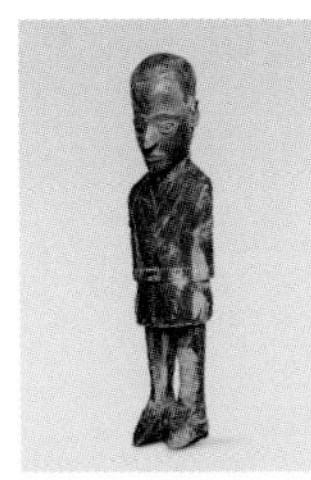

Pl. 42. Chief's or diviner's figure representing a Belgian officer, Kwilu Pende, DRC, 1930s.
Herbert Weiss Collection.
Wood. H.: 62.5 cm.
Naturalism (in three-dimensional sculpture) may also be harnessed to express an aesthetic of astonishment and terror due to its association with portraiture and sorcery.
This unique figure depicts Agent territorial Maximilien Balot, the Belgian officer killed during the 1931 rebellion, in the form of a power object for use in battling the colonial state. Therefore, despite its very different form, this work is equivalent to pl. 41 in its emotional impact.

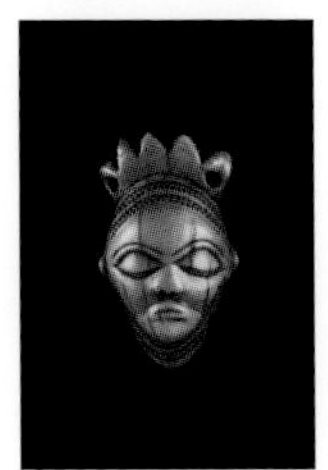

Pl. 43. Ivory pendant, Kwilu or Central Pende, DRC. Félix collection.
Ivory. H.: 9 cm, W.: 5.5 cm.
Pendants in the form of faces always represent masks since sculptors like to avoid any accusations of portraiture, the representation of named human beings, due to its popular association with sorcery. This work likely represents the "mask of the chief" because of its broad face; flat forehead; rounded eyelids; and beard (see pl. 19 and 45).

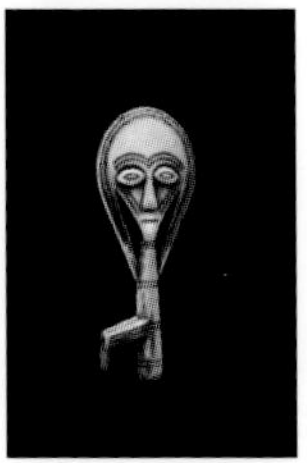

Pl. 44. Anthropomorphic ivory whistle in the form of a key, Kwilu Pende, DRC. Jean-Willy Mestach Collection.
Ivory. H.: 15 cm, W.: 6.3 cm.
Kwilu Pende whistles were popular items of trade with their neighbours, and no wonder. They required the most sophisticated carving skills. Feather-light, this work has a hole drilled through the coiffure so that it can be hung as a pendant. It playfully mimics the form of a European barrel key. As a whistle, one blows across the hollow cylindrical shaft while a finger closes and opens the little hole drilled through the "bit" on the side so that the player can alternate two tones.

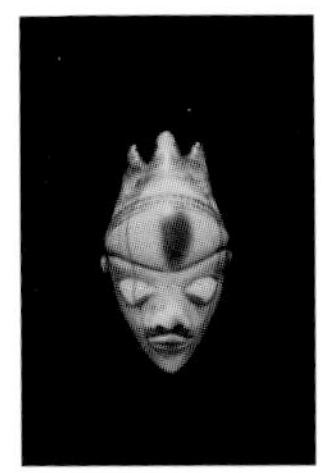

Pl. 45. Ivory pendant, Central Pende, DRC. Collected by Comm. J.-G. Hofman. Royal Museum for Central Africa, Tervuren, EO 0.0.3652; registered in 1936.
Ivory. H.: 6.4 cm, W.: 3.5 cm.
Pendants in the form of Pende masks were extremely popular until Independence as an expression of solidarity and resistance to the colonial state.

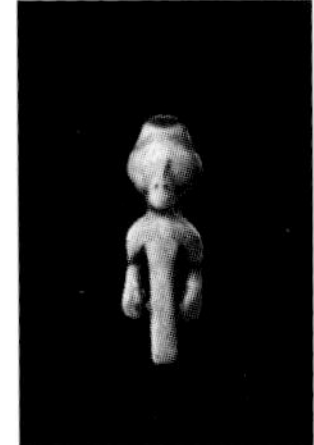

Pl. 46. Ivory pendant, Central Pende, DRC. Udo Horstmann Collection, Zug, Switzerland.
Ivory. H.: 7.8 cm.
In order to inhibit the yellowing of ivory, Pende once scrubbed pendants regularly with abrasive sand, with the result that the features of the face would melt away over time. The transformation of the surface witnesses to the abiding love of the original owner for this small sculpture, who fought for many years to preserve its whiteness.
Once he stopped, the patina emerged.

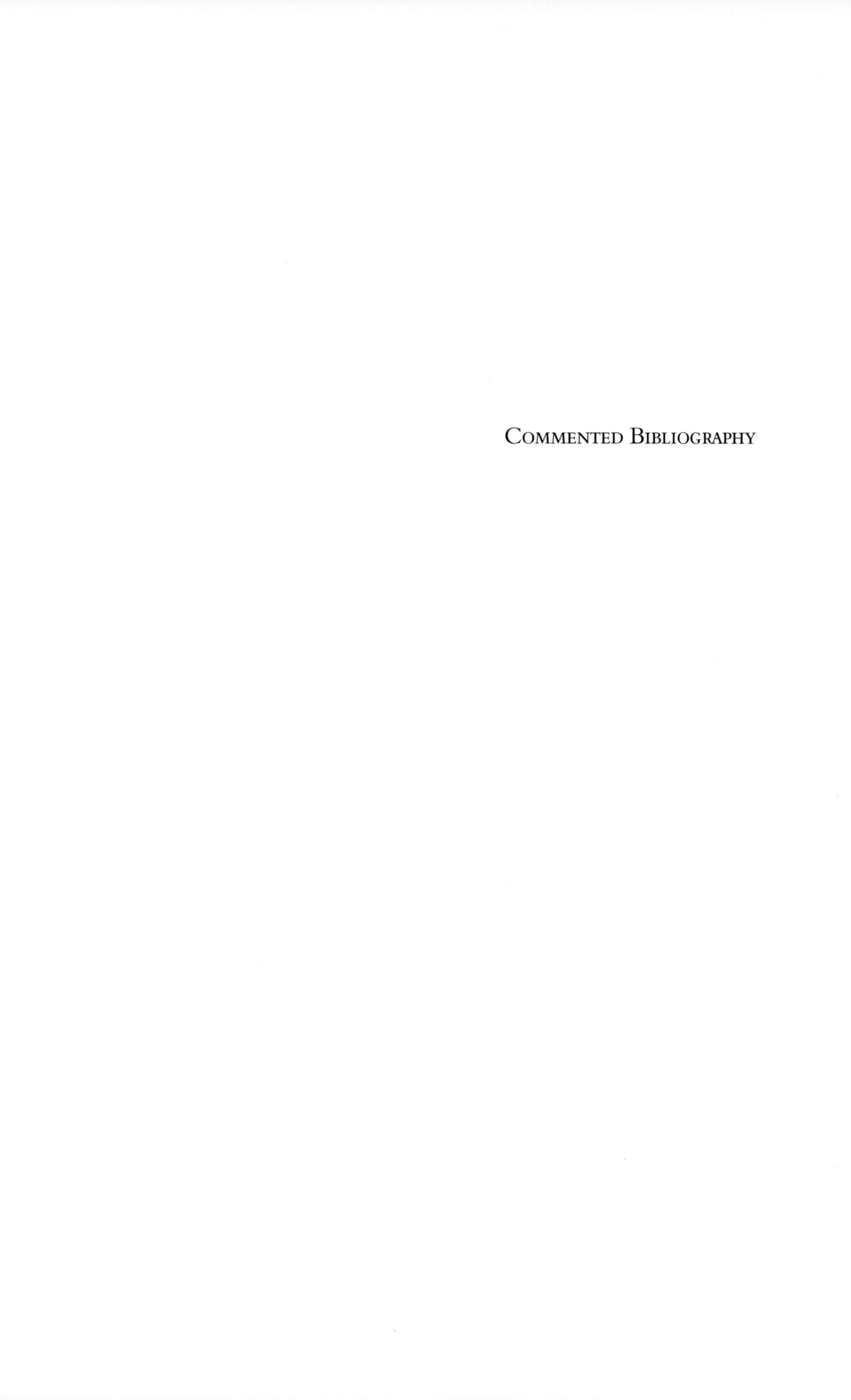

COMMENTED BIBLIOGRAPHY

For a more complete bibliography, see Strother 1998.

Bastin 1994
Bastin, Marie-Louise, *Sculpture angolaise.*
Lisbon: Electa.

"Bâtons de chefs Bapende" 1932
L'Illustration congolaise (Brussels), no. 131 (1 Aug.),
4171. *The earliest description of judicial staffs.*

Biebuyck 1985
Biebuyck, Daniel, *The Arts of Zaïre.*
Vol. 1: Southwestern Zaïre. Berkeley,
L.A.: University of California Press.
An outstanding synthesis of the literature on the Pende
in French, Dutch, and English through 1979.
This text is particularly valuable for placing the Pende
in relationship to their neighbours and for suggesting
many points of cultural continuity.

Bocola 1995
Bocola, Sandro (ed.), *African Seats.*
New York: Prestel.

CEEBA (Centre d'études ethnologiques
de Bandundu)
Since Independence, many Congolese have been
encouraged to write student memoirs documenting various
aspects of their culture. During the 1970s and 1980s,
Hermann Hochegger, the director of CEEBA,
published a number of these essays, which are uneven
in quality since the authors received little formal training.
At their best, they provide a rich mine of documentation
rooted in a particular community (e.g., Muyaga).
However, others require some caution since their
authors do not cross-check their sources and tend
to over-generalise. They are listed under the names
of the individual authors.

Cole 1989
Cole, Herbert M., *Icons.* Washington, D.C.:
National Museum of African Art, 130-31.

De Carolis 1930
De Carolis, "Us et coutumes indigènes:
la circoncision", *Le conseiller congolais*, 3rd year,
no. 1 (Feb.): 47-48.
Rare, early account of the Central Pende men's initiation.

Delaere 1942-45
Delaere, Jacques, "*Nzambi-Maweze*: Quelques
notes sur la croyance des Bapende en l'Être
suprême", *Anthropos*, 37-40, fasc. 4-6: 620-28.
An excellent overview of Pende religion.

de Sousberghe 1954
de Sousberghe, Léon, S.J., "Cases cheffales
sculptées des Ba-Pende", *Bulletin de la Société*
Royale Belge d'Anthropologie et de Préhistoire
65, 75-81, plus 8 pages of illustrations.
One of the most important texts on precolonial
architecture in Central Africa.

de Sousberghe 1956
de Sousberghe, Léon, S.J., *Les danses rituelles*
mungonge *et* kela *des ba-Pende (Congo belge).*
Brussels: Académie royale des sciences coloniales,
Classe des sciences morales et politiques, Mémoires
in-8°, new series, tome 9, fasc. 1 (Ethnographie).
Invaluable interpretation of Lunda funerary rituals
preserved among the Central and Kwilu Pende
as a secular dance society.

de Sousberghe 1959
de Sousberghe, Léon, S.J., *L'art pende.*
Brussels: Académie royale de Belgique,
Mémoires in-4°, 2d series, vol. 9, fasc. 2.
De Sousberghe documents Pende visual culture
from 1907 (the time of Emil Torday's collection)
to 1957 and concludes that one must discard
the idea of a single, homogenous Pende style in favour
of a multitude of local centres. His own fieldwork took
place Sept. 1951-Sept. 1953 and Dec. 1955-1957.

de Sousberghe 1960a
de Sousberghe, Léon, S.J., "Cases cheffales
du Kwango", *Congo-Tervuren* 6, no. 1: 10-16.
Comparative information on sculpted chiefs' houses
in Angola (1957).

de Sousberghe 1960b
de Sousberghe, Léon, S.J., "De la signification
de quelques masques pende: *Shave* des Shona,
et *Mbuya* des Pende", *Zaïre* (Brussels) 14 (5-6),
505-31.
Inspired by M. Gelfand's work on the Shona,
the anthropologist hypothesised that the Giwoyo

and Muyombo masks evoke the image of long-bearded
missionaries from the Kingdom of Kongo (p. 529).
This is de Sousberghe's most speculative treatise.

de Sousberghe 1960c
de Sousberghe, Léon, S.J., "Noms donnés
aux Pygmées et souvenirs laissés par eux chez
les Pende et Lunda de la 'Loange'".
Congo-Tervuren 6 (3), 84-86.
Documents the Central Pende mask Mazumbudi.

de Sousberghe 1961
de Sousberghe, Léon, S.J., *Deux palabres d'esclave*
chez les Pende (Province de Léopoldville, 1956).
Brussels: Académie royale des Sciences
d'Outre-mer, Classe des sciences morales
et politiques, Mémoires in-8°, new series,
tome 25, fasc. 5 and last.
Provides important information on the use of judicial
staffs during trials.

de Sousberghe 1963
de Sousberghe, Léon, S.J., *Les Pende: aspects*
des structures sociales et politiques.
Tervuren: Musée royal de l'Afrique centrale, Classe
des sciences humaines, Annales, series in-8°, no. 46.
The mature statement of the author's ethnography
among the Pende (excepting works of art).
It is concentrated on the Kwilu chieftaincies
and contains a surprising amount about the Lunda
enclave of Mwaat Kombaan, drawing on his friendship
with Joseph Kisefu, the chief's son.

de Sousberghe and Mestach 1981
de Sousberghe, Léon and Jean Willy Mestach,
"*Gitenga*: Un masque des Pende".
Arts d'Afrique noire 37: 18-29.

Duncan 1995
Duncan, Carol, *Civilizing Rituals: Inside Public Art*
Museums. London: Routledge.

Farr 2001
Farr, Michael, *Tintin: the Complete Companion.*
San Francisco: Last Gasp, 66.

Fabian 1998
Fabian, Johannes, "Curios and Curiosity:

Notes on reading Torday and Frobenius".
In Enid Schildkrout and Curtis Keim (ed.).
The Scramble for Art in Central Africa, 79-108.
Cambridge: Cambridge University Press.
The author establishes the early commodification of art
in the Congo and provides a welcome perspective on
Frobenius' collecting methods among the Pende in 1905.

Frobenius 1907
Frobenius, Leo, *Im schatten des Kongostaates*. Berlin.
A brief account of Frobenius' visit among
the Eastern Pende in 1905.

Frobenius 1988
Frobenius, Leo, *Ethnographische Notizen*
aus den Jahren 1905 und 1906 (ed.) Hildegard
Klein. Vol. 3: Luluwa, Süd-Kete, Bena Mai, Pende,
Chokwe. Stuttgart: Franz Steiner Verlag Wiesbaden.
Invaluable documentation of architecture and visual
culture from 1905. The Chokwe had temporarily
pushed back the Eastern Pende into the northernmost
corner of their territory, where Frobenius visited them.

Gusimana wa Mama n.d.
Gusimana wa Mama [=Bartholomé Gusimana],
"Attributs cheffaux des chefs Pende",
Collection Afrique, no. 15. Manuscript.
Library of Congress, Wash., D.C.

Gusimana wa Mama [=Bartholomé Gusimana] 1968
Gusimana wa Mama "L'homme selon
la philosophie pende". *Cahiers des Religions*
africaines (Kinshasa) 2:3 (Jan.), 65-72.
Overview of Pende religion.

Gusimana wa Mama [=Bartholomé Gusimana] 1970
Gusimana wa Mama "La révolte des Bapende
en 1931 (Souvenir d'un témoin)",
Cahiers Congolais de la Recherche et du développement
(Kinshasa) 16 (4) (Oct.-Dec.), 59-69.
An evocative eyewitness account of the 1931 rebellion.

Haveaux 1954
Haveaux, G.L., *La tradition historique*
des Bapende orientaux.
Brussels: Institut royal colonial belge,
Section des sciences morales et politiques,
Mémoires, Coll. in-8°, tome 37, fasc. 1.

A circle of doctors working for the diamond consortium,
Forminière, became cultural enthusiasts of the Eastern
Pende. Haveaux lived for twenty years in the Kasaï and
compiled this important history, citing named informants.

Himmelheber 1993
Himmelheber, Hans, *Zaire 1938/39: Photographic*
Documents on the Arts of the Yaka, Pende,
Tshokwe and Kuba. Zürich: Museum Rietberg.
A selection of fashionable Pende hairstyles
and jewellery, 1938-39.

Hoet 1936
Hoet, Paul, "Mikotto", *Jezuieten Missies,*
2 (May), 134-39.
The most complete account of the men's hairstyle
represented in sculpture by Kwilu Pende and Mbala.
The author remarks that the mikotto *came back*
into vogue following the 1931 rebellion as a gesture
of resistance (p. 139).

Homberger 2003
Homberger, Lorenz, "Vom Ritual zur
Unterhaltung". In *Masken: Gesichter aus anderen*
Welten. Zürich: Museum Rietberg, 82-87.
Good colour reproductions of a series of early masks,
including three Eastern Pende masks collected
in the 1930s, with remarkable preservation
of their original coloration.

Kochnitzky 1953a
Kochnitzky, Léon, "Masques géants,
masques en miniature", *La Revue coloniale belge,*
8 (174) (1 Jan.), 53-55.
One of the first articles popularising Pende art
in the colonial press.

Kochnitzky 1953b
Kochnitzky, Léon, "Un sculpteur d'amulettes
au Kwango", *Brousse* (Léopoldville), n.s., no. 3:
cover and 9-13.
Rare discussion of the mid-century market for ivory
pendants. Important documentation of the celebrated
Central Pende sculptor Gabama a Gingungu.

Kodi Muzong Wanda 1976
Kodi Muzong Wanda, "A Pre-Colonial History
of the Pende People (Republic of Zaïre)
from 1620 to 1900". Ph.D. Dissertation,
Northwestern University.
A superb cultural history. Kodi's base was
in the Lunda enclave of Kangu (Kwilu Pende).

Kopytoff 1986
Kopytoff, Igor, "The cultural biography
of things". In Arjun Appadurai (ed.)
The Social Life of Things, 64-91. Cambridge:
Cambridge University Press.

Kramer 1993 (1987)
Kramer, Fritz, *The Red Fez: Art and Spirit*
Possession in Africa. New York: Verso.
Inspired by de Sousberghe's speculation (1960b)
that certain masks may represent Europeans.

Lema 1982
Lema Gwete, "Art populaire du Bandundu".
In *Sura Dji: Visages et racines du Zaïre.*
Paris: Musée des Arts Décoratifs, 51-77.
Illustrates some masks from the collection
of the Institut des musées nationaux du Zaïre.

Lengelo 1980
Lengelo Guyigisa, *Mukanda, l'école traditionnelle*
Pende. Bandundu, Zaïre: CEEBA
(Centre d'études ethnologiques), 2d series, vol. 59.
A rare text addressing the role of the minganji
during the Kwilu Pende mukanda *(the boy's initiation),*
which declined precipitously during the 1930s.
The author seems to be based on the Lunda frontier.

MacGaffey 1988
MacGaffey, Wyatt, "Complexty, Astonishment
and Power", *Journal of Southern African Studies*
14 (2): 188-203.

Maesen 1975
Maesen, Albert, "Un masque de type 'Gitenga'
des Pende occidentaux du Zaïre",
Africa-Tervuren 21, no. 3/4: 115-16.
Announces a new museum acquisition.

Maquet 1953
Maquet, Jean-Noel, "Initiation à la musique
congolaise". *Jeunesses Musicales* 21 (Dec.): 1-3.

Maquet 1954a
Maquet, Jean-Noel, "La musique chez les Bapende".
Problèmes d'Afrique centrale (Brussels), fasc. 26, 299-315.
An excellent overview of instruments and genres of songs.

Maquet 1954b
Maquet, Jean-Noel, "Anthologie folklorique:
Initiation à la musique congolaise", *Micro
Magazine*, 10th year, no. 468 (28 Mar.): 8-9.
*Part of a series of broadcasts given on Belgian National
Radio, the text is a unique resource for whistles.*

Maquet, M. 1937
Maquet, M., "L'herminette des chefs dans le
district du Kwango". *Les arts et métiers indigènes dans
la province de Léopoldville*, Nov., fasc. 3: 1-3 and cover.
Important early description of the uses of adzes by chiefs.

Maquet-Tombu 1953
Maquet-Tombu, Jeanne, "Arts et lettres:
le sculpteur Mupende Kabamba",
Bulletin de l'Union des femmes coloniales,
no. 142 (25ᵉ année, juillet): 16-17.
*Important documentation of the celebrated Central
Pende sculptor Gabama a Gingungu.*

"Masques Bapende (Kasai)" 1932
"Masques Bapende (Kasai)", *L'Illustration
Congolaise* (Brussels), no. 130 (1 July), 4086, 4091.
*The earliest overview of Central Pende masquerading
and pendants. (At this date, the "Kasai" province
included the Central Pende.)*

Mathy 1953
Mathy, Rose-Marie, "Chez les Bapende, la calebasse:
ses usages et sa décoration", *Bulletin de l'Union des
Femmes coloniales*, issue #142 (25th year, July): 17-18.
Well-researched note on the art of calabashes.

Mudiji Malamba Gilombe
(=Théodore Malamba-Mudiji) 1979
Mudiji Malamba Gilombe, "Le masque pende
giwoyo du musée de l'Institut supérieur
d'archéologie et d'histoire de l'art de l'Université
catholique de Louvain", *Revue des archéologues
et historiens d'art de Louvain* 12, 169-93.
*Essential reading on one of the most widespread
of Pende masks.*

Mudiji Malamba Gilombe
(=Théodore Malamba-Mudiji) 1989
Mudiji Malamba Gilombe, *Le Langage des masques
africains*. Kinshasa: Facultés catholiques de Kinshasa.
*The Abbé Professor Mudiji's theoretical approach
to Pende masks and mukanda draws on structuralism,
psychoanalysis, and phenomenology.*

Muyaga 1974
Muyaga Gangambi, *Les masques pende de Gatundo*.
Illustrated by Tshiamo a Muhenge. Bandundu,
Zaïre: CEEBA (Centre d'études ethnologiques),
2d series, vol. 22.
*Records significant information on the masqueraders,
their costumes and dances, around Mukedi
(Central Pende). Muyaga is the first to document
the indigenous name for an important subcategory
of village masquerading (mbuya jia mafuzo)
and to list a lion's share of the masks included within it.*

Ndambi 1975
Ndambi Mun'a Muhega (=Ndambi Munamuhega)
1975 Ndambi Mun'a Muhega, *Les masques pende de
Ngudi*. Translated by Kamizelo Kikotshi. Illustrated
by Binia Binalbe-Talo. Bandundu, Zaïre: CEEBA
(Centre d'études ethnologiques), 2d series, vol. 23.
*Ndambi's account of the masks is particularly useful
in documenting audience reception and in its focus on the
masking traditions of one region (Ngudi). However,
readers should be alerted that the author does not make
distinctions between eye-witness accounts, third-hand
accounts, and outright speculation inspired by song texts.
Because he did not interview the practitioners, his accounts
of the redoubtable mbuya jia mafuzo are particularly
misleading. The French translation should also be used
with caution. For example, the translator renders
"feathers from the Lady Ross's violet turaco and African
gray parrot" as "feathers of parrots, turkeys, and ducks"
(pp. 214-15)! (See notes on CEEBA).*

Ngolo 1976
Ngolo Kibango, *Minganji: Danseurs de masques
Pende*. Bandundu, Zaïre: CEEBA (Centre d'études
ethnologiques), 2d series, vol. 35.
*An important source on the Minganji, the masks
associated with the mukanda (boy's initiation
and men's fraternity), which declined radically during
the 1930s among the Kwilu and Central Pende.*

Nicolaï 1963
Nicolaï, Henri, *Le Kwilu: étude géographique*.
Brussels: Centre scientifique et médical de
l'université libre de Bruxelles en Afrique centrale.
An extraordinary study that treats the Kwango-Kwilu
region as an integrated environmental, economic
and cultural unit. The text analyses the colonial
impact on architectural practice and provides many
beautiful perspectival drawings and plans for specific
buildings as well as a few village maps.

Olbrechts 1982 [1946]
Olbrechts, Frans M., *Congolese Sculpture*. Trans.
Daniel Crowley and Pearl Ramcharan-Crowley.
New Haven (Conn.): Human Relations
Area Files.

Ombredane 1952
Ombredane, André, "Les techniques
de fortune dans le travail coutumier des noirs",
Présence africaine 13: 58-68.
Documents the construction of a single house in Dongo.

Palata Fulgence Duval 1957
Palata Fulgence Duval, "'Mbuya': Le masque
Tundu". *Echos de Gungu* 1 (July-Aug.): 11.
Recounts the form and performance of the Central
Pende clown mask.

Petridis 1999
Petridis, Constantine, "Tree Altars,
Spirit-Trees, and 'Ghost-Posts' Among
the Luluwa and Neighboring Peoples".
Baessler-Archiv 47, 115-50.
Situates Pende cephalomorphic posts
in a regional context.

Petridis 2002
Petridis, Constantine, "Mbala, Tsaam,
or Kwilu Pende? A Mother-and-Child Figure
from the Kwango-Kwilu Region
of the Democratic Republic of the Congo",
Cleveland Studies in the History of Art 7, 126-41.
Petridis argues that many Kwilu Pende
sculptures have been misattributed to the Mbala
on the basis of their mukoto *headdress, including*
a ravishing maternity figure in Cleveland.

Rodolitz 2003
Rodolitz, Scott, "Replica or Reference:
A Reassessment of Pende `Ikhoko'."
Tribal Arts 7: 2 (summer), 64-73.
Argues for an amuletic interpretation of ivory pendants.
Beautiful reproductions from the Mestach collection.

Rubin 1974
Rubin, Arnold, *African Accumulative Sculpture*.
New York: Pace Gallery.

Rubin, W. 1987
Rubin, William, "Pende Mask", In *Perspectives:*
Angles on African Art. New York: Center for African
Art, and Harry Abrams, Inc., 58-60.

Rudlin 1994
Rudlin, John, *Commedia dell'Arte*.
London: Routledge.

Schildkrout 1998
Schildkrout, Enid, "Personal Styles and Disciplinary
Paradigms". In Enid Schildkrout and Curtis Keim
(ed.). *The Scramble for Art in Central Africa*, 169-92.
Cambridge: Cambridge University Press.

Scohy 1952
Scohy, André, "Savanes du Kwango".
In *Étapes au Soleil*, 135-73.
Brussels: Aux éditions du chat qui pêche.
The source for many familiar photos.

Sikitele Gize a Sumbula (=Sikitele Gize) 1973
Sikitele Gize a Sumbula, "Les racines de la révolte
pende de 1931", *Études d'histoire africaine*
(Université nationale du Zaïre at Lubumbashi) 5,
99-153.

Sikitele Gize a Sumbula 1976
Sikitele Gize a Sumbula, "Les causes principales
de la révolte pende en 1931", *Zaïre-Afrique*
(Kinshasa) 16, no. 109: 541-55.

Sikitele Gize a Sumbula 1986
Sikitele Gize a Sumbula, "Histoire de la révolte
pende de 1931". Ph. D. Dissertation,
Université de Lubumbashi, 3 vols.
In probing the causes of the Pende rebellion, the author

compiles a magisterial encyclopedia of Kwilu Pende
culture, ca. 1930. He reprints long passages
from many archival documents, which are now difficult
or impossible to retrieve.

Strother 1993
Strother, Z.S., "Eastern Pende Constructions
of Secrecy", *Secrecy: African Art that Conceals*
and Reveals (ed.) M. Nooter. New York:
Center for African Art, 156-78.
Explores issues of visibility for the arts surrounding
*the chief's ritual house (*kibulu*).*

Strother 1995
Strother, Z.S., "Invention and Reinvention
in the Traditional Arts", *African Arts* 28:2 (Spring),
24-33, 90.
Argues for the adoption of popular culture methodology
in studying masquerade through the invention history
of the Central Pende mask, Gindongo (gi)tshi?

Strother 1998
Strother, Z.S., *Inventing Masks: Agency and History*
in the Art of the Central Pende.
Chicago: Univ. of Chicago Press.
Beginning with the premise that performers invent masks,
the text examines the codes of physiognomy that allow
sculptors to match the "face" with the dance. It also traces
an art history of masquerading from the precolonial
period to the waning days of the Republic of Zaïre.

Strother 1999
Strother, Z.S., "Gabama a Gingungu
and the Secret History of Twentieth-Century
Art", *African Arts*, 32: 1 (Spring), 18-31, 92-93.
This essay explores the changing position
of Pende artists from 1870 through the 20th century
and assesses the impact of the international
market on their sculpture.

Strother 2000a
Strother, Z.S., "From Performative Utterance
to Performative Object: Pende Theories
of Speech, Blood Sacrifice, and Power Objects".
RES: Journal of Anthropology and Aesthetics 37
(Spring), 49-71.
How is making a power object among the Pende
(and by extension Central Africa) akin to writing a letter?

Strother 2000b
Strother, Z.S., "Smells and Bells: the Role
of Skepticism in Pende Divination".
In *Insight and Artistry* (ed.) John Pemberton III.
Washington, D.C.: Smithsonian Institution Press,
99-115, pl. 8-9.
Examines the ambivalent representation
of diviners in masquerade. The essay argues
that a deep scepticism about diviners has fuelled
a dynamic market for new techniques and art forms.

Strother 2002
Strother, Z.S., "Iconoclasm by Proxy".
In Bruno Latour and Peter Weibel (eds.),
Iconoclash: Beyond the Image Wars in Science,
Religion and Art. Cambridge (Mass.):
MIT Press, 458-59.
Argues that putting objects in harm's way comprises
a form of iconoclasm.

Strother 2004a
Strother, Z.S., "Architecture Against the State:
The Virtues of Impermanence in the *Kibulu*
of Eastern Pende Chiefs in Central Africa".
Journal of the Society of Architectural Historians
63: 3 (Sept.), 272-95.
Detailed analysis of the ritual house of Eastern
Pende chiefs. The essay argues that the ephemerality
of the house (and its related sculpture) is part
of a strategy to curtail political ambition.

Strother 2004b
Strother, Z.S., "Dancing the Heat of Life".
In Frederick John Lamp (ed.), *See the Music,*
Hear the Dance. Munich: Prestel, 88-91.
Detailed examination of the performances
of Pota and Ginjinga.

Strother 2005
Strother, Z.S., "La perte et l'efflorescence:
Paradoxes de l'histoire de l'art colonial
dans le Pende central". In *La mémoire du Congo.*
Le Temps Colonial, Jean-Luc Vellut et al (eds.).
Ghent: Editions Snoeck, 115-19.
Attributes a second mask to Gabama a Gingungu
and reviews the impact of the colonial period
on Pende art history.

Strother 2007
Strother, Z.S., "Léon de Sousberghe (Obituary)."
African Arts, 40:2 (summer), 8-11.
Discusses the conditions for research
on the arts in the 1950s.

Torday 1907
Torday, Emil and T.A. Joyce, "On the Ethnology
of the South-Western Congo Free State".
Journal of the Royal Anthropological Institute 37,
133-56, plates 17-20.
Torday travelled in an ethnically mixed area
bordering on the Kwilu Pende in 1906
and his confusion has been transferred directly into
the art literature. For example, he conflates "Bapende"
and "Bapindji". ("Pindji" is the pejorative Pende
term for enclaves of Mbuun-speakers. These people
call themselves "Mpiin".) The Bakwese that he describes
are now classed as Pende. His best information
came from Chief Yongo (whose successor aided Léon
de Sousberghe).

Torday 1922
Torday, Emil and T.A. Joyce, *Notes ethnographiques*
sur les populations habitant les bassins du Kasaï
et du Kwango oriental. Tervuren: Musée du Congo
Belge, Ethnographie, Annales, 3d ser.,
vol. 2, fasc. 2. *The best record of Torday's travels*
and collections along the northern frontier
of the Kwilu and Central Pende, 1906-1909.

Van Braeckel 1994
Van Braeckel, Hilde, "Pende fluwelen:
geborduurd of geweven?" *Vlaamse Vereniging voor*
Oud en Hedendaags Textiel. Bulletin. 37-54.
Unique examination of Pende textile techniques,
arguing that early "Kasai velvets" were woven rather
than embroidered. Beautiful diagrams.

Van Coppenolle and Pierson 1982
Van Coppenolle, Renée and René Pierson,
Bapende: Contes - Légendes - Fables. Waterloo:
Les Dominicaines de Fichermont.
Pierson made this important collection
of Central Pende stories around the mission
of Kilembe from 1938-1946.

Vanden Bossche 1950
Vanden Bossche, Adrien, "La sculpture de masques
Bapende", *Brousse* (Léopoldville), no. 1: 11-15.
Documents the technique of sculptors. As curator
of the Musée de la Vie indigène de Léopoldville,
the author became an important promoter
of contemporary Pende art.

Vanden Bossche, J. 1950
Vanden Bossche, Jean, "Le film au service
de l'Ethnographie". Brousse (Léopoldville)
1950 (1), 5-8.
The source for the influential interpretation
of Pende masquerading as a kind of Commedia
dell'Arte, based on types, which Kochnitzky (1953b)
later developed and popularised.

Vanden Bossche, J. 1966 [1951]
Vanden Bossche, Jean, "L'Art plastique
chez les Bapende", *L'art nègre.*
Paris: Présence africaine, 143-47.
The first true overview of (Central) Pende art.

Vanderstraeten 2001
Vanderstraeten, Louis-François, *La répression*
de la révolte des Pende du Kwango en 1931.
Académie royale des Sciences d'Outre-mer.
Classe des Sciences morales et politiques.
Mémoire in-8°, Nouvelle Série, tome 53,
fasc. 1. Brussels.

Verly 1959
Verly, Robert, "L'art africain et son devenir".
Problèmes d'Afrique centrale, 13th year,
no. 44: 145-51.
Important documentation of the renowned Eastern
Pende sculptor, Kaseya Tambwe. As Director
of the Ateliers Sociaux d'Art indigène du Sud-kasaï,
Verly was an important promoter of Eastern
Pende sculpture.

Vidler 1992
Vidler, Anthony. *The Architectural Uncanny.*
Cambridge, MA: MIT Press.

Wissmann 1974 (1888)
Wissmann, Hermann et al., *Im Innern Afrikas:*
Die Erforschung der Kassai während der Jahre 1883,

1884 und 1885. Nendeln: Kraus Reprint.
The most substantial record of pre-colonial life.
Lt. Hans Mueller visited the Eastern Pende in 1884.
He penned an evocative account of Pende villages
perched on hilltops or nestled among luxurious palm
groves. Mueller's record of his difficult negotiations
with Chief Kombo ("blind, an old man, weary of life")
dovetails perfectly with oral history describing the blind
Matshiobo-a-Nguanya (Chief Kombo-Kiboto)
as too old and tired to flee with his people
when the Chokwe attacked a few years later.
This is also an important early source for raffia textiles.

Z.S. Strother is Riggio Professor of African Art
at Columbia University in the City of New York.
She was trained in art history at Yale University,
where she received her Ph.D in 1992. Since then,
she has published extensively on African visual culture, including *Inventing Masks: Agency and History
in the Art of the Central Pende* (University of Chicago
Press, 1998), which received the Arnold Rubin
Outstanding Publication Award for "original schol-
arship and excellence", 1998-2000. This research is
based on 32 months of fieldwork among the Eastern
and Central Pende, 1987-89. A short follow-up study
(Dec. 2006-Jan. 2007) has allowed her to assess some
of the impact of fifteen years of turmoil on the arts in
the Democratic Republic of the Congo. Her current
research focuses on untangling the history of iconoclasm in Africa.

Colour Separation
Eurofotolit, Milan

Printed in Italy by Bianca & Volta, Truccazzano, Milan
for 5 Continents Editions, Milan